Crazy

CW00746683

A Nov(_

by
Mark Rickman

FOR GERAINT ROBERTS
BEST WISHES
Mark Rickman

Circaidy Gregory Press

Crazy Bear

Copyright Information

ISBN 978 1 906451 19 6

Printed in Great Britain by the
MPG Books Group, Bodmin and King's Lynn

Published by Circaidy Gregory
Creative Media Centre,
45 Robertson St,
Hastings,
Sussex TN34 1HL

www.circaidygregory.co.uk

Chapter One

'But of course you're going to have a flat warming, darling,' my sister-in-law purred from somewhere behind the complicated mix of coloured threads attached to her embroidery frame. 'How can you move into your lovely new flat and not have a flat warming?'

Crazy Bear rises catlike to his moccasined feet, folds his mighty arms, and stares coldly down at the woman now crouched in terror, her hands raised skyward in supplication. 'Foolish one,' he rumbles from somewhere deep inside his massive chest, 'Cease your clack and hear me. This sorrowing chief without squaw must carry his blankets from four bedroom wigwam with garage and gardens front and rear in Mitcham to three room shithole with carport in Cheam and you say I have flat warming? You sick in head.'

Aloud I said, 'I'm only moving from the house to a small flat, Delia. I really don't want a lot of fuss making.'

Delia lowered the embroidery frame and clicked a disapproving tongue. 'It's not a lot of fuss-making to meet your new neighbours, is it? It's not a lot of fuss-making to invite a few old friends over for a farewell drink, is it?'

A few old friends? Crazy Bear drops a battle scarred hand on to the bloodstained shaft of his tomahawk and narrows his eyes to slits. Would that be old friend Richard who swung round a lamppost and pushed open the letterbox flap to scream happy new year to a dying woman? Or could it be the ones who've been crossing the road and staring in shop windows rather than find a few words to say to the poor sod of a bereaved husband? If they're the ones, of course I want them at my flat warming. With a bit of luck, they'll choke on their cocktail sausages.

Closing one eye, Delia squinted down at the embroidery frame, licked her lips and guided her stubby needle up through the printed canvas and down again. I watched the length of scarlet thread appear, loop, disappear, and grow shorter with every stitch. When it disappeared for the last time and my sister-in-law stopped clacking on about sausage rolls and canapés and became fully occupied in selecting and licking a new length of thread, I meant to tell her politely and firmly where to stick her flat warming.

Thank you Delia, I was going to say, but no thanks. I'd rather creep in to the flat when no one's looking and eat pigshit.

I lost the chance to say anything at all when halfway through the length of thread, she asked who I was going to invite. I stared at her and took out a handkerchief to wipe my eyes.

'Oh for Heaven's sake, Michael,' she said snappily. 'You've got to stop brooding. Of course you'll have a flat warming. You need to get over yourself and start meeting people. You're only forty three. It's important you don't become a recluse.'

Important I don't become a recluse? What is a recluse, I wanted to know. If it's someone who crawls into a corner to die, lead me to it. If they teach reclusery in evening classes, I'll join tonight.

Delia clicked her tongue again, put down the embroidery frame, and said, 'Michael, are you listening to me?'

'Listening to you?' I repeated. 'Of course I'm listening to you. You want me to have a flat warming.'

'Honestly, darling, I've gone on miles from there. I was saying you spend too much time alone. It'll do you good to meet some new people.'

'People as in woman? Now that my wife is dead and cremated, you want me to find a new woman to shag? I'd sooner make love to my hand.'

'That is disgusting!' Her front teeth dug into her lower lip. 'I ought to tell your brother some of the things you say to me. I bloody would if he wasn't so sorry for you. It's just that he thinks…'

'I know what Bobby thinks,' I shouted and had the moody satisfaction of seeing her flinch. I held up my hands in apology and ploughed on, 'I'm sorry Delia but I know what you and Bobby think. The boys think the same. Go ahead with the flat warming, if you think it's such a good idea. Ask anyone you like. I have to go now. It's getting late.'

Delia put the embroidery on a table and rose gracefully to her feet. Brushing down the front of her dress, she gave me one of her understanding smiles. 'Why don't you stay and eat with us, Michael? Bobby will be home in half an hour.'

I shook my head. 'Not tonight, if you don't mind. I've got my dinner waiting in the flat. You know what Margery used to say? It's a shame to waste good food.'

2

'I know,' said Delia, 'Of course I remember. Do you want anything to take with you? Milk, bread, anything at all?'

I shook my head again. 'No, I'm fine, thanks. Really I am. I've got plenty of everything.' I walked to the door, knowing she was watching me. When I reached it, I turned and said awkwardly, 'I'm sorry if I upset you, Delia. I don't know why I say things sometimes. I never mean any of it.'

Delia shrugged and stood on tiptoe to put her hands on my shoulders and kiss my cheek. 'Just remember we love you, Michael,' she said as I left the house.

'Hey, do you remember that one?' I asked Crazy Bear as we crossed the Madden Road and walked towards Cheam and the new flat. 'That's the party trick Margery and I used to pull on the boys when they were small. Stop crying, George, stop crying Dicky, Mummy and Daddy love you. Show us where it hurts and we'll kiss it better.'

Only kissing it better doesn't work. I spent all night trying it on Margery. In the morning I was kneeling by her bed with my head on her pillow and my eyes closed when the little fair haired doctor followed a nurse through the screens, put her hand on my shoulder, and said, 'It's all over, Mr Brent. Mrs Brent has passed on. You have to come away now, Mr Brent. She isn't yours any more. She belongs to us now. There are things that have to be done that can only be done by doctors and nurses. You can come back and see her after we've made her presentable for you. Mr Brent. Please!'

I could hear the doctor's voice getting higher and scratchier. I could smell her perfume. I could feel her sharply pointed fingernails digging into my shoulder. I tried to get to my feet and go with her but my knees had stiffened and one of Margery's eyes was half open and looking at me and I couldn't stop saying, 'I love you Meg. Show me where it hurts, my lovely girl. I'll kiss it better.' The doctor's voice became a hysterical squeak in my left ear and her nails were digging deeper but I couldn't let go of Margery's hand and I couldn't stop trying to kiss it better. Begging her to wake up and live happy ever after but she couldn't do it. Not even for me. After a time, the doctor gave up and the boys were sent for.

George and Dicky lifted me to my feet and half carried me through the screens and out of the side ward. They held my arms when I struggled to get back. After a while I stopped fighting and

3

was glad of their support. They took me through double doors and into a corridor while the fair haired doctor and two nurses did to Margery whatever it was doctors and nurses did for dead people. My sons sat me on a bench outside an office and through the crazy buzzing in my head, I thought about Margery who was thirty eight years old and too young to be dead. And I thought about me, a year older and too young to be left alone.

The door was a faded light blue and badly scratched where keys had spent years scrabbling around for the lock. Above the keyhole was an incongruous and highly polished brass knob. The walls of the corridor were beige and brown and smelled of sick and disinfectant. Between my feet lay shiny, chevron patterned brown lino tiles. People walked past me without speaking. Some drifting towards the wards as though afraid of what they would find in them. Others walked more briskly as they made for the glass doors at the end of the corridor happy to be free of the hospital gloom, happy to be anonymous, lost among the crowd in the busy sunlit street.

Tucked away at the back of a wardrobe at home was a rarely worn dark suit and tie. I had no black shoes. Which was Margery's fault. She didn't like me in black anything. But there was no help for it now. She was dead, there was going to be a funeral, I had to have a pair of black shoes. The buzzing in my head increased its volume, I was desperately tired after spending the night holding Meg's hands in both of mine, but I got jerkily to my feet and followed the people walking through the glass doors into the street. Blinking in the clear morning light, I rubbed a hand across my scrubby face and saw a shoe shop on the corner of the roundabout.

'Can I have a pair of black shoes, size nine, wide fitting please,' I said to the woman who rose from a chair as the shop door opened.

'Don't cry, my love,' she said. 'For the love of God, don't cry.'

Delia and Bobby took care of the death certificate, the funeral arrangements, and the letter from the Inland Revenue telling me I would now be taxed as a single man. Meaning to be kind, they took away Margery's clothes, shoes, handbags, gloves umbrellas, and make-up case. They took the bottle of perfume I bought for her last birthday. It was a mistake. They left an empty wardrobe and nothing to touch. Nothing to glorify. I needed to glorify the dead Margery. To prove to myself she was perfect and at peace with God. Any niggling reminders of squabbles we had over TV programmes, the children's education, or washing up after dinner had to be suppressed or remembered as my fault. The Margery I needed to create at the start of my long period of whisky-soaked mourning was without fault.

'Why don't you care about the boys?' a suddenly aggressive Delia asked, about a year after the funeral. 'It was hard enough for them to lose their mother, they shouldn't be losing their father too. It was Dicky's birthday last week. You didn't even send him a card.'

'Of course I care about the boys,' I mumbled at her through the bottom of my glass. 'They're my sons aren't they? George and Dicky know I care about them. You and Bobby know I care about them. Everybody knows I care about them. I forget birthdays, that's all. It's not a crime, is it?'

Delia cut through my rambling. 'How do they know you care? How do Bobby and I know? You never say anything to them. You never talk to any of us.'

'What do you want me to say to you, for Christ's sake? I don't know the language any more.'

Delia pulled a face and turned to my brother. 'Tell me what he's going on about,' she demanded. 'I never know what he's talking about when he gets into one of his moods.'

Me get into one of my moods? Bobby or no Bobby, Crazy Bear's hand is on her throat and she is hung out for the birds to peck at while he is through the front door with her bloody scalp held high in one hand. Howling his triumph at the sky, the chief leaps on the back of his pony, presses his naked thighs and calves against the warm barrel of its chest, and gallops with the wind to hunt the eagle for another golden feather. There was no need for Delia to remind me about George and Dicky. I knew the wrong parent died. The boys would know how to deal with a grieving mother. They'd kneel beside the pathetically weeping old girl and kiss her on the cheek. They'd say you've got us Mum. You've always got us.

Who was going to kneel beside a pathetically weeping old father and give him a kiss? Who would tell him, 'you've got us, Dad. You've always got us'? No one. No one tried. I don't know what I'd have done if they had tried. Delia was right. If I couldn't talk to the boys, it meant I'd stopped caring. Maybe I never cared. I wanted them to be all right. I'd be pleased if they were happy. But care? I couldn't care the way Margery cared. I wasn't the one who fed and watered and rubbed them down with an oily rag when they needed it. Who was I to expect feedback? When did they ever get anything worth having from me apart from the chances of Wimbledon for the cup?

Crazy Bear reins in the pinto and throws back his head to scream, 'When?' at the Blue Hills and my sister-in-law. 'When, Delia? Can you hear me, Delia? What do you think of this for disgusting, Delia?' He slides to the ground, pulls out his magnificent cock, and pees rich and golden against a rock. 'What about this, Delia?'

Chapter Two

The arm waving imagery of a shouting match with my sister-in-law came to an end when I found myself outside my new block of flats, saying hello to one of my new neighbours who was washing his car.

'Hi, Vic,' I said. 'It seems I'm having a flat warming next week.'

He looked up from the bucket he was wetting his leather in, saw my face, and laughed. 'Never mind, mate. With a bit of luck the flats will burn down. Then you won't have to bother.'

I shrugged and tried to return the smile. 'It's my sister-in-law's idea. I don't know who else is coming but I'm relying on you and Joan for a couple of friendly faces.'

Vic laughed again and threw his bucket of water over the car to rinse off the suds. 'We'll be there, you can rely on it. My old woman will do anything for a free drink.'

'Been looking for a lady like that for years,' I said as I left him and began climbing the stairs.

'Sorry mate,' Vic called as he started to leather the bonnet. 'She's spoken for.'

'The best always are,' I called back as I opened the front door, stepped over the small heap of letters on the mat, and to Crazy Bear's total disgust, poured myself a drink and began to cry.

Despite what I told Delia, there was no food in the flat. Not that that was anything to worry about. With a fish and chip shop on one corner and a sandwich bar on the other, I'd be hard put to starve. On the other hand, Vic had begun to polish his car and I didn't want to face him again. I poured another drink, tucked myself into the corner of the sofa and had my favourite set pattern nightmares.

It is April 14th, the night before I am to deliver Margery to the hospice. Chemotherapy has left her hair wispy and sparse, her face is drawn, loose lipped, and hardly recognisable, her voice reduced to a whisper. She can no longer support herself sitting or standing. She smells strongly of the surgical spirit the District Nurse and I rub on her elbows, back and heels to prevent bedsores. When she is uncomfortable or in pain, she rings a cheap little hand bell so that one of us will lift her higher on her pillows or support her on the commode.

The nightmare is at its worst. I can't take any more. I have just closed my eyes and the bell is starting to jingle again. There is no way I can drag myself off the sofa. Yet somehow I must have for when I force my eyes to open, my arms are close round her and our noses are almost touching. We are looking deep into each other's eyes and some dark thing she sees in mine makes her whisper, 'Don't hate me, Michael. You mustn't hate me.'

I can't say the right words. How can I make her understand that I don't hate her, I could never hate her? I hate the cancer that riddles her body, befuddles her brain, and has become part of her. I hate the fact I no longer know how to separate the two parts. I lift her higher on the pillows, she searches my eyes, and still I can't speak. At last she turns her head away and her whisper is so low I have to strain to hear it. 'Take me to the hospice, Michael.'

'N-no Meg,' I stutter in the voice I find too late. 'You don't need the hospice. I'm here. The nurse comes every day. We look after you.'

Her eyes are closed. 'Take me to the hospice, Michael.'

'I love you!' I shout to make her look up at me. 'I don't want you to go to the hospice. I don't want to lose you. I don't want you to die.' But her head remains turned away and I know that tomorrow I will take her to the hospice. Not even tomorrow. Behind the partly drawn curtains the sky is brightening and birds are taking up the dawn chorus. In ten days Margery will die and there will be nothing left for me to hate but every morning's brightening sky and dawn chorus.

'Please don't hate me, Michael. You mustn't hate me,' Margery is whispering as I struggle out of the dream and four years of my life are gone somewhere. I am sitting on the old sofa I insisted on bringing with me to the flat. Much to the disgust of my sister-in-law, who is shaking my shoulder hard enough to spill my drink.

'What the hell.' I begin as whisky slops over the edge of the tumbler.

'It's getting on for flat warming time, Michael,' Delia says brightly. 'Aren't you going to change? Your guests will be arriving soon.'

'Sod them,' I said.

Chapter Three

Selling the house in Mitcham and moving to the flat in Cheam was never my idea. But as Delia and my brother had been pleased to remind me at every opportunity, the garden was overgrown, the blocked guttering splashed water all over the front door, and there was an inexplicable stain on the sitting room wall. My sons had moved out two years earlier, the dog the boys named Woocus Superbus and Margery called Wookie had died, and the cat was living next door. When I wasn't eating with Delia and my brother, I lived on take aways that upset my stomach because I'd buggered up the oven timer and couldn't be bothered to get it put right. Bobby walked round the house with pursed lips and said I'd best get an estate agent in before the house had to be sold as in need of renovation. It wasn't the only thing in need of renovation, I could see my sister-in-law thinking as she looked at my scruffy old cardigan and worn trousers.

If Delia wanted a flat warming she could get on with it without me. I sat tight on the old sofa I first saw in Margery's bedroom a few weeks after we became engaged. She'd taken me upstairs to look at some of our wedding presents and, not daring to mess up the bed, we made love on the sofa, with her hand over my open mouth to stop me yelling. I patted her side of the sofa for the memory and gulped my drink while on the other side of the room people I didn't know came in and said hello before taking nuts and crisps from Delia and a drink from Bobby. Then, like every party I'd ever been to, they stood talking to the people they came in with and looking at the shit colour wallpaper I promised I'd change while more people I didn't know came in and did the same. I topped up my drink and was steadying it with both hands when Delia brought a couple of them over to me. 'You don't know this one, darlings,' she said to them. 'He is Michael, your friendly host and new neighbour.'

To me she said, 'Michael darling, these are Tony and Clare. They live on this level in the next block.'

'Really?' I asked as though it was the most incredible news I was likely to hear in my life. 'You live in the next block? On this level?'

9

'We most certainly do,' squeaked Clare, throwing herself on the sofa and bouncing where Margery would curl up and tuck her icy feet inside my cardigan. 'Our bed's on the other side of your bedroom wall, so no listening please.' She giggled before going on, 'We brought you a pretty little cut glass vase from Pratts for your flat warming. I do hope you like it, Michael dear. It's the blue one in the Debenhams bag.' I held my glass steady against her bouncing and thought how she'd best get her fat arse off Margery's sofa before I smacked her silly face.

'Would you care to see it?' asked Tony. He was big and soft, with a smooth pink fudge face and a small wet mouth set low among his chins. I didn't like the look of him and I didn't have the faintest idea of what he was talking about.

'See it?' I asked, looking at the small wet mouth.

'The cut glass vase from Pratts, Michael old chum. We think it's rather sweet but we can change it if you absolutely hate it.'

'Oh, the vase from Pratts.' I sat back and smiled up at him. 'No, I've no need to see it now. I'm sure the two of you have impeccable taste. Thank you, Tony and Clare. Thank you very much indeed.' I continued to smile at Tony, wanting to tell the fat, unhealthy looking slug that I'd just moved out of a four bedroom house full to the brim with cut glass vases, fruit bowls, table lamps, and all the rest of the dust-collecting gubbins my wife and I accumulated over God knows how many years. Did he have the faintest idea how much of my life I threw away just to fit into this sodding little shit hole of a flat. What did I want with their fucking cut glass vase? They could shove it where the monkey shoves his nuts.

I beamed and raised my glass to show Tony how grateful I was to have a cut glass blue vase from Pratts in a Debenhams bag while Clare resumed her bouncing and squeaked, 'Is that your brother serving the drinks, Michael dear? He's awfully like you, isn't he? And so generous with the gin. I'm a little squiffy already.'

She was wearing a white wispy nothing much of a dress. As she bounced, her unfettered breasts bobbed up and down to a different rhythm to the rest of her body and the hem of the nothing much dress rose up from two inches above her knees to the top of her thighs. Out of the corner of my eye, I could see the blue shadowed swell behind the fork of her tiny white briefs and I hadn't had any for a very long time. I shut my eyes and let myself see a chopped and bloodied Tony tied to our old apple tree while a whooping Crazy Bear mounted a naked Clare, her breasts bobbing up and down to a rhythm of their own. It was the wrong vision and, panicking, I opened my eyes and made myself concentrate on Tony.

'My wife would have loved the vase. She liked glass,' I gabbled. 'She learned to etch. Pictures of grapes and leaves and twisty ivy and things. She went to evening classes every week. She got so interested in etching on glass, I could never find anything to drink out of. I sometimes got home and found she's forgotten to make supper for me and the boys.'

'Really?' said Tony. 'Etching grapes and leaves and ivy on glass. How very interesting. Isn't that interesting, Clare?'

'Oo yes.' Clare smacked her thin red lips and crossed her legs, secure in the knowledge that I could have fucked her on the spot. 'It must be ever so interesting. Etching on glass.'

I turned away, finished my drink, and reached for the bottle I kept in a place of safety behind a cushion. Glaring at Delia when she leaned over and took it from me.

'We can't have you getting sloshed before you've met everybody, darling,' she said. 'You've hardly spoken to a soul.'

'Course I have,' I protested. 'What about Tony and Clare? They were here two minutes ago. I was talking to them only two minutes ago.'

'Honestly darling, that was yonks ago. They're over there talking to that nice man Vic from the flat downstairs.'

'Two minutes,' I insisted. Looking across the room at Clare, I dropped my voice to a stage whisper. 'Here, you know what she is, don't you?'

Delia laughed. 'Probably better than you do, darling. I think you'll be safer talking to Vic. He says you've already become quite good friends.'

'Vic,' I shouted. 'Bring a couple of drinks over and have a chat. Delia says I haven't talked to anyone in yonks.'

'Here' he repeated, handing me a glass and sitting on the sofa beside me. 'What's yonks?'

'My sister-in-law's got a language of her own and don't get your hopes up. She eats little men like you and me for breakfast.'

Vic raised his eyebrows. 'Hot blooded, is she? I'll have to try my luck next time the missus is at one of her evening classes.' He

11

swallowed a little whisky and thumped the worn arm of the sofa with the flat of his hand. 'Nice solid piece, this. I don't blame you for hanging on to it.'

'Yes,' I said; looking at a spurt of dust lifting from the spot he'd hit. 'It was my wife's. I taught the boys to do headstands on it.'

And Margery was sitting on it the evening she told me the typewriter wasn't working. I'd got home late from the factory where I'd had a blazing row with a bloody minded quality controller who should have been checking out a docket of coats so I could get the delivery vans loaded and off to the warehouse instead of wasting everybody's time arguing the toss about a few crooked labels and a couple of hanging cottons. When I walked in, Margery was tucked into the corner of her sofa with her hands between her knees. I took my coat off and muttered something dirty at her and she said accusingly, 'I thought you had that typewriter fixed last week. The blooming thing's useless.'

'Then I'll take the mucking thing back in the morning,' I snapped. 'You don't have to look at me like that. It's not a bloody tragedy, is it? What's for dinner?'

'You try it,' she said. 'You should have tried it in the shop.'

I glared at her. I'd had a hell of a day. I hadn't got over the row I'd had with the quality controller, there'd been no time for lunch, my belly was rumbling, my head ached, and I needed this crap about a lousy typewriter like I needed a hole in the head.

'Now look,' I began angrily but Margery wasn't looking anywhere. Her head was hanging and tears were dropping on to the backs of her hands. Suddenly afraid of what I was seeing, I put my hand on her shoulder and said, 'Come on Meg, don't do that to me. You know what I'm like when I've had a bad day.'

'Please, Michael,' she said.

I sat at the old manual typewriter she filched from my office a couple of years earlier and two-finger typed, 'This is to warn Margery Brent that if her old man doesn't get his dinner in the next thirty seconds, he is going to make mad passionate love to the first bag of crisps that walks past this house attached to a woman.' Taking the sheet of paper from the machine, I held it out.

'Don't,' she said, 'I know it's me. I can't feel my left hand. I keep dropping things.' Taking her hands from between her knees, I held them against my face and kissed the palms.

'They feel pretty good to me,' I told her. 'Where are the boys, upstairs?'

Margery nodded.

'So how will it be if I send George for some fish and chips and a couple of pickled cucumbers while I give the doctor a ring?'

Margery nodded again. When she finished nodding, her head drooped and her hands went back to being pressed between her knees. I sat beside her, stroked her hair back from her forehead, and tried to laugh it off.

'I know what it is, you soppy ha'porth. You can't bear feeling ill. You never could. Don't worry so much. The good old doc will fix you up.'

'Will he, Michael?' She glanced sideways at me and in that instant, I knew he wouldn't. And we both knew there was nothing wrong with the bloody typewriter before ever I sat at the desk.

'We've got ourselves a bit of a pinched nerve, my love,' the good old doc said while he ran his pudgy fingers up and down the back of Margery's neck. 'We're as stiff as a board. Been driving with our window down, have we?'

Margery looked sheepish for a moment and then grinned. 'Maybe we have,' she told him loftily. 'We really can't remember.'

Doctor Brennan laughed, winked at me, and said, 'Shame on you, Margery Brent, making fun of an old man. You'll be old yourself one day.' The good old doc was wrong on both counts. Margery didn't have a pinched nerve and she never got the chance to grow old.

Beside me, Vic cleared his throat and thumped the arm of the sofa for a second time. I jumped and said I was sorry, I must have been miles away and would Vic say it again, please. He indicated the crowded room. 'Small wonder you can't hear me with all this racket going on. I was saying it's a good piece of furniture. They don't make them like this any more.'

I shrugged. 'I expect they do but my wife was fond of it. She would kip down on it while the boys and I watched telly. Then she'd get me to make her a cup of cocoa because she wasn't sleepy enough to come up to bed.' Vic laughed and said I could have been talking about his Joan.

I shook my head. 'There couldn't be two like that. It's impossible.'

'They're all like that,' said Vic. 'Low lives the lot of them. But we'd be hard put to manage without them.' He stopped suddenly and put a hand on my arm. 'I'm sorry, mate, that was stupid. I wasn't thinking.'

I smiled at him. 'It's all right, Vic,' I tried to say through the dark memories of the tumour pressing on Margery's brain, the operation in the Atkinson Morley, the chemo-therapy in the Royal Marsden, the pretty young woman with a dragging leg falling into my arms as she tried to walk past me with the knowledge of death in her eyes. 'It's all right, Vic, I'm getting over it.'

Together we watched Delia bring a youngish woman across to us. 'Look who just dropped in,' she said brightly. 'My old school chum, Sara Leighton.'

'Hi,' said Vic while I stared at the newcomer, 'Come and join us. There's always room for a pretty girl.'

'Thank you, kind sir,' said Sara, perching on the arm of the sofa where Margery wouldn't let anyone sit. 'I went to Delia and Bobby's house and was told to come on here for a flat warming. Hi, Michael. What were you and Vic looking so serious about?'

'Do we know each other?' I asked.

'I was one of Margery's bridesmaids but I wouldn't blame you for not remembering. I was twelve years old and so shy and gawky, you'd have had to look behind Delia to find me.'

She smiled at me. It was a nice smile but I wasn't fooled. We were all the way back to where Delia wanted me to meet new people. People in the shape of Sara Leighton. I shook my head at the thought and said nothing. From somewhere behind me Crazy Bear farted to show his contempt. Vic laughed and looked up Sara.

'You don't look shy or gawky to me,' he said, 'but I expect Michael had other things on his mind at the time.'

'Why don't you go and talk to the other young people?' I asked her. 'You don't want to waste your time on a couple of old fogies like us.'

'Hey,' said Vic, his cheeks scarlet. 'You speak for yourself.'

I had another drink and slurred over saying, 'All right, an old fogie like me.' But when I looked up, Sara Leighton was gone. Vic was gone. Everyone was gone. I thank God and curl up on Margery's sofa, lay my head where I can still sense her presence and enter the safety of my own private nightmare. The bell is jangling. I can't take

14

any more. Behind the partly drawn curtains the sky is brightening, and birds are taking up the dawn chorus.

Chapter Four

Next morning I fell out of the single bed I had bought to remind me that a phase of my life was over, crunched over my partygoers' dropped crisps and nuts to the shower, and turned it on full blast. Joan, I vaguely remembered, had promised Delia she would come up to the flat and help tidy up. I, I vaguely remembered, had promised Delia I wouldn't touch a thing and, apart from the nearly full, now empty bottle of whisky I took to bed with me, I hadn't. My head splitting, I was getting out of the shower promising Jesus, Joseph, and Mary I would never touch another drop when Joan let herself into the flat with my spare key, surveyed me and a skimpy towel in dripping near nakedness, and began to laugh.

'I was going to tap on the bedroom door and ask if you were decent,' she said, 'but I don't think I'll bother.'

'Too blooming old to be anything but,' I croaked as I wrapped a dressing gown round myself and made for the bedroom. 'I'll be with you in a few minutes.'

'Don't you try kidding me, Michael Brent,' she called after me. 'I saw the way you were drooling over Clare next door last night. Oh yes, and you can stop telling my old man he's past it. You'll be ruining what's left of my love life.'

'I'm sorry, Joan,' I apologized through the door as I towelled myself down. 'I didn't mean to upset Vic. I was trying to get rid of that ruddy woman who was hanging round us.'

'Sara Leighton? I don't know why you would want to get rid of Sara. Vic and I both took to her. We think she's nice.'

By the time I'd found my clothes and joined her in the kitchen, she was washing glasses and stacking them on the draining board.

'Hi again, Joan,' I said, kissing her on the cheek and reaching for a wiping up cloth.

'Hi yourself,' she said, taking the cloth away from me. 'I'll do it this once. You go and make your peace with Vic. If you say the right thing, he might give you a spot of breakfast instead of the clip round the ear he said you were asking for last night.'

'I'll try to charm him. Once upon a time I was rather good at charming people. Once upon a time I charmed Margery.'

Joan had put down one glass and picked up another before she said quietly. 'You ought to stop feeling quite so sorry for yourself, Michael. It really doesn't suit you.'

'What would you say to a kipper?' Vic asked when I put my head round the door to apologize.

'I'd say I'm sorry mate, I couldn't look you in the eye this morning. A piece of dry toast and a dozen aspirin in aspic will do nicely, thank you.'

Vic chuckled and pulled out a chair for me. 'It serves you right for having a skinful last night. Sit down and have some toast and marmalade. You need something to line that suffering stomach of yours.' He ate his grilled kippers while I nibbled on toast and Joan's home made marmalade in a companionable enough silence. I had reached the second slice and third cup of black coffee stage before I said awkwardly, 'Thanks a lot for the breakfast, Vic, and I really am sorry about the nonsense I spouted last night. It was the drink talking.'

Shrugging, Vic said, 'It doesn't matter a toss what you say to me, even if I didn't much care for it at the time. What I don't understand is why you were having a pop at Sara Leighton. She seemed a nice enough young woman to Joan and me.'

'I know,' I said as I accepted another cup of coffee and reached for the sugar bowl. 'The plain truth is, she seems a nice enough young woman to me, too. Maybe I'm not ready for nice young women yet. I don't know what to do with them.'

'Come on sunshine, your memory's not that bad. It's like riding a bicycle.'

'I can buy sex if I want to. I don't need someone like Sara Leighton for a bit of the other.'

Vic reddened. 'I wasn't talking about sex. All right, I know it's part of what's what but a man needs a bit of company too. I think you need someone you can spend some time with. Besides, having a girl friend might help you cut down on the booze and that wouldn't hurt, would it?'

I forced a laugh. 'You two believe in straight talking, don't you? First Joan tells me to stop feeling sorry for myself and now you're talking to me as though I'm an alcoholic.'

Reaching forward to pat me on the shoulder, Vic grinned at me. 'That's what we say to your face, my son. You should hear what we say behind your back.'

Thanking him again for the breakfast, I ran downstairs, reversed the car out of the garage, and drove through Croydon on to the Brighton Road. Dumping it in a layby, I walked across the downs wishing I still had the dog to shout 'come back here you stupid bugger and leave those bloody bitches alone' to. I wished I'd brought a hip flask with me. I wished I could get my mind to start thinking straight. Joan and Vic were right. Delia was right. Everybody was effing right. I had let myself get scruffy. I was sorry for myself. I drank too much. I drank alone. If Delia wanted to introduce her to me, Sara Leighton looked like a nice young woman. Not just the bit of grumble and grunt I thought I was looking for. And I ought to stop poncing about in a field of wet grass and go back to work. With my partner, my brother, and my very good friend Bobby who made far too many allowances for me.

Bobby, who felt as sorry for me as I did. Bobby, who had to do my job as well as his own now that Margery's death had turned me into a useless piece of crap. It was what Delia kept telling the two of us, either separately or as a pair. Bobby was being good to me instead of being good for me and he was working himself into an early grave because of it. As for me, Delia said with her hands on her hips, it was high time I pulled myself together and stood on my own feet. She said I couldn't go on mourning forever. I'd had a bad time but I've been through the mourning period. It was time to take the next step.

Christ, as if I didn't know! I stopped in my tracks and looked at a group of kids flying brightly coloured kites. Trying to anyway. One ran at me desperately trying to get his kite off the ground. A kite that seemed perfectly happy to bump along behind him, achieving nothing.

'Try running downhill you daft little bugger,' I wanted to tell him. 'Get up a bit of speed.' Pretty much what Delia was telling me. Get on with it. Get up a bit of speed. Let's see a bit of action.

If only I could. I'd been mourning Margery from the time she was taken ill, never mind since she died. I didn't know how to stop mourning. I didn't know how to take the next step. I didn't know what the next step was. What was I supposed to do for Christ's sake.

18

Put her away? Tuck her photograph in a drawer and forget she was ever there? Get myself a new woman, get myself a new life and forget the memories? If that was what it took, I couldn't do it. I could never forget Margery. It wasn't histrionics. I could never forget her because consciously or subconsciously, she was the part of me I thought about every day. What she would have done, what she would have said, what she would have called me if she caught me on the booze after I promised her and the rest of the world I would lay off.

'Oh bloody hell,' I said, having to turn my head away from the panting child and his obstinate kite and almost walking into a passing couple who were being dragged along by a pair of bouncy yellow Labradors.

'Think of something else. George and Dicky, Delia and Bobby, Joan and Vic, Sara Leighton. They all liked Sara Leighton, didn't they? I hadn't disliked her. I wouldn't have picked a fight if she hadn't parked her fat derriere on the arm of Margery's couch. Except she didn't have a fat derriere. Or did she? I thought about it and remembering it as quite a nice bum, decided I wouldn't have minded patting it the way I used to pat Margery's, and had to laugh at what I was thinking. The couple I'd passed with tears in my eyes had turned back with their dogs and were looking at me curiously.

'They'll have you put away, my son,' I said to myself while the couple put as much distance between themselves and me as they could. 'That's what nice ordinary sane people who walk their dogs on the downs do to nutters like you.' I laughed again. Maybe Sara Leighton would be the answer to my problems. Companionship and sex. I remembered sex. Like Vic said, it was like riding a bicycle. Sex could stop me being so bloody maudlin. Sex could stop me being alone so much. Sex could stop me boozing.

I hurried back to the car thinking if those two caught me crying again they'd really send for the men in white coats. So far as Sara Leighton was concerned all I had to do was wait for the world-famous Delia follow-up to a party. Once she started something, my darling sister-in-law left nothing to chance. She would telephone me before the day was out. I knew exactly what she'd say. First she'd waffle on about how much she and Bobby enjoyed the flat warming and what wonderful neighbours we had with the possible exception of Clare who was a nasty little prick teaser if ever she saw one and I simply must do something about that dreadful wallpaper. Then she

19

would hope that Bobby hadn't given away all my booze and I still had a nightcap if I really needed it, though she'd prefer a nice cup of cocoa herself, hint and hint hint. Casually she would drop in the welcome news that her very dear friend Sara Leighton had enjoyed meeting my friends and me. And then she'd say, 'as a matter of fact, darling, I'm thinking of giving a small dinner party myself one evening soon. I thought I might ask Sara and perhaps you would like to make up a four.'

'And when you ask, my dear old darling Delia,' I said aloud as I drove back to the flat, 'I'm going to shake you rigid by saying yes please, I'd love to make up a four with Sara Leighton. Or a two. Or anything else she might have in mind.'

On the way home I bought sandwiches, milk and cornflakes and, turning my back on Crazy Bear's mounting impatience, waited two days for the call from Delia. On the third day, I picked up the telephone and dialled her number.

'Michael darling,' she shrieked a little too brightly even for Delia. 'I've been meaning to call you for days. I don't know where the time goes, do you?' I didn't answer and she plunged on with, 'Wasn't it a lovely flat warming? Bobby and I enjoyed it so much. I do hope you've still got a bottle or two in your drinks cabinet after the way Bobby tried to give it all away. And your neighbours are so nice. Except for Tony and Clare perhaps. I should watch myself with that one, if I were you. She is definitely a little odd. What was their cut glass vase like? Oh yes, and who brought in the tray of croquettes? They were delicious.'

I waited until she ran out of steam and then replied that I hadn't yet looked at any of my house warming presents and thanks to her and Bobby getting rid of it to a cheapjack dealer, I no longer had a drinks cabinet, and there weren't any croquettes. That must have been one of the other parties she went to.

'Of course there were croquettes, darling. Joan made them herself and she and Vic brought them up. I like Joan. I like them both.'

'Vic and Joan like you and Bobby too. They took quite a shine to that little friend of yours, Sara Whatsaname. I hope she enjoyed the party as much as everyone else did judging by the amount of booze and nuts they knocked back?'

Delia hesitated. 'Well no, Michael. My little friend Sara didn't enjoy the party as much as I hoped she would. She took it in her head I was trying to pair the two of you off but honestly darling, I only wanted what was best for you both.'

'What the hell makes you think you always know what's best for other people?' I snarled before I slammed the phone down and instantly regretted the action. I didn't know what the fuck I was getting so worked up about. It wasn't as though I was interested in Sara Leighton. I didn't give a sod about Sara Leighton. The reason I was angry was because that silly cow Delia kept pushing me into these bloody stupid situations. Now Joan and Vic were at it as well and once again, I'd made a fool of myself.

'I'm all right as I am and bugger the lot of you,' I was saying to Delia and Bobby and Joan and Vic and the whisky bottle in my hand when the phone rang.

'She called you that sad man!' Delia flung at me. 'Is that what you wanted to hear? Sarah said she didn't want to get involved with that sad man. I'm sorry, Michael. I'm so sorry.' Shocked, I listened until I heard her drop the telephone back in its cradle. If she had screamed at me or swore or clicked her tongue, I'd have thought nothing of it, her temper was as quick as my own. But she was crying.

'Stop doing that, you silly cow,' I said to the dead telephone. 'You don't cry. I'm the one who cries.' Feeling sick and knowing the blood had drained from my face; I topped up my drink and took it into the bedroom. Gulping at the whisky, I choked a little, swallowed some more, and for the first time in nearly four years, had a good look at myself in the almost full-length mirror on the wardrobe.

Over a crumpled tee shirt, I was wearing the same baggy, food stained cardigan and unpressed trousers I wore on the night of the flat warming. Seeing what Sara Leighton had seen, I could hardly blame her for calling me sad. My hair, streaked with grey, badly needed cutting. My eyebrows lowered defensively over eyes that looked as though they'd had no sleep in a month or more. A pinched look around the nostrils and the down turned petulant mouth completed an air of despondency so completely that even I could manage a rueful laugh. Holding up my glass, I toasted my reflection, swallowed the rest of the whisky to prove I was still my own man, and walked out of the flat and into the High Street to spend some money.

The next morning I screwed up my courage without recourse to the whisky bottle, bought a couple of bunches of flowers, and took them to Delia.

'I didn't mean to upset you, Delia,' I said lamely. 'I'm very sorry.'

She took the flowers from me with both hands, carefully put them on a hall table, and moved into my arms. 'Darling Michael, I didn't mean to hurt you either. You know I'd never want to hurt you.' With her face buried in my jacket, she sniffed and said dreamily, 'Umm, you smell good enough to eat.'

Stiffening, she pushed me to arm length, stared for a long moment, and then pulled me to her for another kiss. 'Thank God,' she said softly. 'Oh thank God.'

I couldn't help preening a little. 'What do you think of the new jacket?'

'You idiot,' she laughed. 'It's bloody awful.' And she kissed me again.

Chapter Five

I stood at the gas stove frying my breakfast eggs and tomatoes and day dreaming about throwing the sheets back, climbing into bed and saying it's your old man, who were you expecting, and Margery putting her head on my shoulder and saying I was getting a bit bony in my old age and someone else might make a nice change at that and me sliding her pyjama trousers down and putting a hand beneath the curve of her naked rump to lift her to me and say it wasn't bones, I was Genghis Khan taking time off from the heat of battle and in too much of a hurry to strip off my chain mail and this was no time for her to be telling me she'd lost the key to her chastity belt again. Margery was smiling up at me, accepting me, her breath uneven as she fitted her love making to mine when the telephone rang, making me jump half out of my skin and nearly set fire to my dressing gown knocking the frying pan off the stove.

Assuming it was yet another bloody minded double glazing salesman ringing at precisely the wrong moment, I snatched up the telephone and snapped, 'Michael Brent.'

'Sara Leighton,' she snapped in return. 'I rang to thank you for the flowers, Mr Brent. Goodbye.'

'Hey!' I yelled. 'Hang on a minute. What flowers?'

There was a pause and just as I was thinking she'd put the phone down, she said quietly, 'Delia, of course. I should have known she was up to her old tricks.'

'Look,' I said, 'if you're talking about the woman my brother loves, what has the silly cow done this time?'

I'd heard Sara Leighton speak warmly to Vic and I'd heard her angry with me. This time the voice was a stranger's, cool and impersonal. 'I'm sorry to have troubled you, Mr Brent. I had a rather silly tiff with your sister-in-law and she sent me a bunch of flowers with a note that read 'I'm sorry for the misunderstanding, Michael Brent'. Since you obviously know nothing about it, I'll return them to her.

'No,' I said hurriedly, 'please don't do that. You're not the only one who can fall out with Delia and I bought the flowers for her. Why don't you keep them as a peace offering from both of us? My sister-in-law can be an idiot but most of the time, she means well.'

'You mean her heart's in the right place?'

'Exactly,' I said gloomily. 'The problem is knowing where she buries her head.'

Sara Leighton had a nice laugh. I chuckled with her and chanced my luck with, 'I'm not going to the factory today. Can I give you lunch?'

'Why would you want to give me lunch?'

'So you come and rub belly like Eskimo Nellie,' roared Crazy Bear. 'You ruin chief's breakfast, it's the least you can do.'

'You made me ruin my breakfast,' I said. 'It's the least you can do.'

'It will have to be in Croydon. I can meet you a little after twelve thirty.'

'Outside Debenhams? I know a pretty good restaurant around the corner.'

Sara hesitated. 'I prefer a vegetarian. Will that be all right?'

'You can eat anybody you like,' I said generously. 'So long as I don't have to look at your plate.'

I waited for the click of her receiver before I replaced my own, made a soggy sandwich of the cold eggs, took a cautious bite, put it down, and put the kettle on. Holding a mug of coffee in both hands, I perched on the kitchen table and congratulated myself on still having the ability to chat up a bird. After which, I began to wonder. Why had I offered to buy her lunch? Not just for the pleasure of watching her eat, that was for sure. Crazy Bear was right. I was getting restless. The move from the house to the flat. The Spring sunshine flooding through the kitchen window. Even the row with Delia over the stupid bloody flat warming. It had all served to unsettle me and make me realise how badly I needed Margery and since I couldn't have Margery, someone like her. A woman to hold in my arms and talk rubbish to. To walk along a towpath with and look at the boats. To enjoy a play or a concert with. To laugh and cry with. To come back to life with. To rub bellies like Eskimo Nell with.

Leaving the ruins of my breakfast in the kitchen bin, I walked into the bathroom, dropped my dressing gown on the floor, and turned on the shower.

'To rub bellies with,' I repeated into the water cascading over my head and shoulders. 'You silly old sod. Still going on about sex. Bloody, bloody sex.' I'd been celibate far too long. Not just since

24

Margery died. Much earlier than that. Any physical lovemaking had to stop when she became ill a year earlier and never came back. It wasn't that I hadn't wanted it. During her illness and even before she died there had been times when I curled up on the sofa beside her bed and thought of nothing else. After she died and left me alone, there were nights I drove myself silly fantasizing about the proverbial golden-hearted tart who would understand and comfort me, maybe even be a little in love with me while she helped me bury myself deep inside her voluptuous body.

The truth was, I was forced to admit when I got out of the shower and began to towel myself down, I wouldn't have known a golden-hearted tart if she hit me in the eye with her G-string. So where else does a lonely man go for a bit of a nibble? Sara Leighton, maybe? I wondered about her while I shaved and dressed. Since Delia brought her to my flat warming, she had to think there was a distinct possibility. Or would be when I knew Sara Leighton well enough to mention the little matter of 'your place or mine'. I tried to remember her as she sat on the arm of the sofa, talking to Vic. Nice figure, as far as one could tell in the easy-fitting blue dress she wore. Nice hair too. Soft and with a bit of a curl to it, like Margery's. Hair a man wouldn't be afraid to ruffle. I drew a deep breath and tried to imagine Sara Leighton in the nude, in the bed, but the only face and body I saw was Margery's. And the memory of holding the sick Margery in my arms and lifting her higher on the pillows was the wrong memory.

Not wanting to cry or spoil my new image by drinking, I wrenched my mind back to Sara Leighton at the flat warming. When she'd more or less told me to go stuff myself, she said she wasn't that young. About thirty, I'd have guessed. Which was hardly likely to make her a virgin in this day and age. Or any other day and age, I supposed while I took two brushes to my newly trimmed hair. So who could be more ideal for my first post-Margery having it off, bit of the other? There was no need to rush things. After Sara had eaten her vegetarian and spat out the bones, I might tell her I was a lonely sailor who'd served Queen and country before the mast for thirty years and I'd disembarked from the good ship *Kettle Pettle* so desperate for a bit, I'd had my hair cut and bought a new jacket for the occasion.

'So,' I could ask politely, 'how about taking off your knickers and letting me slip into something comfortable? Or better yet, something exciting?' I was still elaborating on the speech when Joan knocked on the door and asked if I was decent and if so, could she borrow a pint of milk.

'What's mine is yours,' I told her when I opened the door. 'Come on in and give me a kiss. I've been saving all my love for you.'

She blew me a kiss from a safe distance. 'You're bright this morning,' she said, 'but it's no use trying it on with me, you sauce box. I'm spoken for. Why don't you try your luck with that nice girl Vic is so smitten with?'

'If you and Vic think I should,' I answered meekly, 'I suppose I'll have to.'

Joan came over to put a hand on my wrist. 'She really is a nice girl, Michael. It's time your luck changed. You're due for a bit of luck.' And I trod on Crazy Bear's moccasined foot to stop him sniggering.

Sara Leighton looked neat, crisp, and businesslike in a brown linen suit worn over a high necked cream blouse. Not a bit like the well-rounded femme fatale in the low backed black satin slinky I'd half hoped for. She looked a touch startled when I crossed the road to greet her and said, 'You look very nice in that. How do you like my new jacket?'

'Since you ask, not too much,' she replied, cautiously eyeing the over-bold brown and white check as she shook my hand. 'Do you mind if I don't think well of it?'

I shrugged. 'Women have no taste. Delia said it's the sort of monstrosity she'd expect me to buy but anything is an improvement on my favourite cardigan which she ordered me to put in the bin.'

'Having seen the cardigan in question, I'm glad there are still some things your sister-in-law and I can agree on.'

'Great,' I grumbled as I smoothed down an imaginary crease in my sleeve, 'now I can hate the two of you equal.' And Sara Leighton reminded me that she had a nice laugh.

We walked through the pedestrian precinct towards the shopping centre and as we crossed the road, I put my hand under her elbow and tried to imagine I was walking with Margery. I might have kept up the pretence if Sara hadn't led me into a pizza restaurant, neatly exploding the myth. Margery would have dragged me into her favourite Chinese for spring rolls and the lioness's share of a roast duck.

'I'd have taken you into a Chinese restaurant,' I told Sara when our pizzas arrived. 'I don't know if they serve Vegan meals.'

'Most restaurants do these days,' she corrected me, 'but this is vegetarian. There is a difference, you know.'

'No,' I said, suspiciously prodding at the pizza and pretending an interest I didn't feel, 'I don't think I do know. Why don't you tell me?'

I let the explanation go through me or round me and watched her hands. Slim, brown, long fingered hands that had spent the morning typing letters and could now take up a knife and fork, slice neatly through a piece of cheese and tomato pizza, and transfer the food to an equally efficient mouth. Inside which her teeth would chew, her throat would swallow, and her stomach begin to digest while her mind returned to directing the hands. Then the wonderfully simple process eating was for her and the horribly complex problem eating had become for Margery could begin all over again.

I watched Sara Leighton slice, transfer, chew and swallow three or four more times, put down my napkin, scrambled to my feet, and excused myself.

'I could fucking kill you, you stupid thick bastard,' I gritted while I pressed my forehead hard against the cool of the mirror in the restaurant's tiny loo. 'If I thought you were going to make such a bloody fool of yourself, I might have done. She's not Margery. She doesn't have to be Margery. She's just a woman you can talk to and maybe get to know. Maybe even get the bit of the other you keep going on about. Stop playing silly buggers and pull yourself together.'

Ignoring Crazy Bear's foot stomping howl of outrage, I wiped my eyes, walked back to the table, and smiled at the woman who held out the prospect of a bit of the other. 'I'm sorry about that,' I said, carefully not looking at her hands as I sat down. 'Were you really saying Delia went through a vegetarian phase? I don't remember hearing a thing about it.'

Sara looked at me thoughtfully. 'I was telling you we were neighbours when we were children. Since Delia was a few years older than me, my mother asked her to take me to school and bring me back every day. She used to order me about. She told me which school dinners to eat and which subjects I needed to be good at, She even told me what games to play and which teachers to hate the most.'

'And now she's doing the same sort of thing to me,' I said as I forked a wedge of pizza into my mouth. 'She hasn't changed a bit.'

Sara smiled her nice smile and went on eating. She had nice legs too, I noticed. Long and silky and very come hitherish. Encouraged by her come hitherish legs, I cleared my throat and told her that once the boys were old enough to look after themselves of an evening, Margery and I would take off and drive wherever our fancy took us.

I put down my knife and fork and before Sara could interrupt me, began to waffle about how much Meg and I enjoyed those evenings. How much I missed them. How much I would appreciate it if she, Miss Sara Leighton, would come with me some evening. In the near future, hopefully. When she could spare the time. If she liked, we could leave the car at the South Bank and have a coffee in the Festival Hall. Or take a stroll along Riverside Walk and check our watches to see if Big Ben is telling the right time. Or go to the theatre. Or anything else that took her fancy...' My voice began to falter when I saw that she too had stopped eating and was watching me. Raising my eyebrows, I tried to smile and wondered what in hell I'd done wrong this time.

'It's not Miss,' she said quietly, 'it's Mrs. I am Mrs Sarah Leighton, recently divorced and the mother of an eight year old daughter who can't understand why I am forcing her to live in a grotty little flat instead of living at home with her beloved father. Every day Julie tells me she'll never forgive me for taking her away from her beloved daddy and her best friend and making her change schools. In other words, Michael, she's too young to leave alone and too bloody-minded and rebellious to trust with a baby sitter. Are you still asking me to come out with you?'

Do you still have nice legs, I was thinking when I looked into her eyes and said, 'Yes, Mrs Leighton. Of course I am.'

28

Chapter Six

We had a trial run the following Sunday afternoon. Julie, an eight-year-old replica of her mother apart from the child's very fair straight hair, was stiff and unrelaxed, refusing to meet my eyes or to answer when I said hello. When we left the car and began the short walk to the park with the duck pond I promised to take them to, she distanced herself from me as though I was suffering from some highly contagious disease I couldn't wait to infect her with. Sara did her best to divide her attention between us while I couldn't think of a word to say to mother or daughter and Crazy Bear pranced around us, screaming at the sky and deciding which head to bring his axe down on first.

'How about a cream tea before we go down to the pond?' I suggested, hoping to at least crack the ice.

'That would be lovely,' Sara said, smiling gratefully at me. Turning to Julie, she gave a tiny shake of her shoulder. 'Wouldn't that be lovely?' she asked with a touch of desperation in her voice. Trying to give the impression she hadn't heard, Julie stalked into the green and gold restaurant and, finding herself seated opposite me, blushed furiously and looked through the window at the passing traffic until our teas arrived. She ate her jammy scones without looking at her mother or me except once, when I offered her the dish of cream. Her eyes met mine for a moment, went down to the proffered dish, and then slid reluctantly back to the window.

'No thank you,' she said in a prim little voice.

Sara sighed. 'Are you sure you won't have some, Julie? You don't get cream teas every day of the week.'

'I could if I wanted to.' The child's voice was high and thin and full of fear. 'My daddy would give me cream teas every day if I wanted him to. He told me he would.'

'Oh don't be so stupid,' Sara said dismissively. 'You know perfectly well he wouldn't do anything of the sort.'

'Yes he would!' shrilled Julie. 'If I wanted him to, he would.'

I looked at the small flushed face and seeing how near to tears she was, said hastily, 'It really doesn't matter. If Julie doesn't want the cream, I'll finish it myself.'

'Are you sure?' Sara asked suspiciously. 'You haven't had much of it so far.'

'Of course I'm sure,' I lied cheerfully. 'I didn't want you to see how greedy I am, that's all. There's nothing I like more than a good big dollop of cream.' I reached for the dish and hoped against hope that Julie would break down and snatch it first. When she didn't, I spooned the more than generous helping on to my remaining scone and forced it down while Sara drank the last of the tea I had hoped to wash the taste away with.

'You don't know what you missed,' I told Julie, giving her a sickly smile that wasn't returned. I paid the bill while they were in the loo and agreed with the hovering waitress that my little girl was in a funny mood today. She said they get like that sometimes, especially when they're having a funny time at school. Her little girl was the same till it turned out that one of the teachers was bullying her and needed a bit of sorting out. Which she well and truly got. The waitress could tell me a thing or two about schoolteachers who got funny with the kids they didn't take to. I escaped by giving her three times the usual tip and my hand on heart promise that I would take time off work and check the school for funny teachers first thing in the morning. Then I followed Sara and Julie out of the restaurant and into the park. Sara and I dropped into deckchairs and watched Julie dutifully produce a large bag of crumbs. While she wandered off in a vain search for an undernourished duck, I said, 'She's not a bit keen on me, is she?'

Sara laughed ruefully. 'She's not a bit keen on me either. How can I make a child her age understand why I took her away from her father?'

'I know it's difficult,' I said to the despair in her voice. 'I wish I knew what to say to my boys sometimes. Children are never easy. I should think when Julie's old enough, she'll understand the problem. Our marriages can't always work out the way we expect them to.'

'But who will she blame for the breakdown when she does understand there are problem marriages. I couldn't stop her loving her father and even if I could, I wouldn't. It wouldn't be right.' She turned to watch the stiff, lonely little girl walk to the edge of the lake and I could see the longing in her eyes. And the touch of heartbreak when Julie glanced in our direction and Sara waved too late to catch her daughter's eye. I then spent a couple of minutes being harangued by Crazy Bear.

'Foolish one,' the chief rumbled. 'Can you not see squaw think only of papoose and papoose think only of father. Neither wants you. Why don't you behave in time honoured way of English gentleman? Piss off quick while they're not looking.'

'And then what?' I wanted to know. 'Lie on my bed and listen to myself breathing? Anything's better than that. Even this.' Turning to Sara, I said as lightly as I could, 'Oh come on, Julie's only a baby yet. Give her time. She'll get over it.'

'Will she?' Sara replied. 'I wonder. As of now, all I hear from the baby is when are we going home to her wonderful daddy who loves her so much and why didn't I think of that before I took her away.'

I shook my head and watched with her while the child picked her way through the squabbling ducks and scattered crumbs. A boy, smaller and thinner than Julie, smiled tentatively and said a few words to her. She stared at him until he lost the smile, scuffed a shoe in the gravel and, as I might have done at that age, hung his head.

Hearing Sara sigh, I said, 'If this weather keeps up for a few days, maybe you and Julie would like a run down to Brighton next weekend?'

'What would be the point? Why go to all that trouble for us?'

I was thinking of offering her three guesses when I said, 'I was thinking of coming too. It is my car.'

'Idiot,' she laughed and I laughed with her, making Julie turn sharply to look at us.

'Lunch with me on Tuesday,' I said. 'We can talk about it then.'

Sara shook her head doubtfully. 'With her the way she is, I honestly don't think it's fair to saddle you with my problems. Perhaps you can find someone less committed.'

'Perhaps I can, but I like being with you. I enjoy your company. If it's all right with you, we can lunch together once or twice a week and take Julie out when there's a free weekend. We might even spend the occasional afternoon together when she's in school.'

'And do what? Go to the library?' I met her eyes and admitted that the library wasn't quite what I had in mind.

'Of course not.' She turned her head to watch Julie again. 'I really would think about looking for someone else, Michael. I don't think this is going to work out the way you would like it to.'

'Sara Leighton,' I said patiently. 'I have three overdue books to return to Sutton library. If you promise to stand between me and the librarian when she looks at the date stamps, I'll buy you a vegetarian sausage and salad mess next Tuesday.'

Sara managed a smile, leaned back in her chair, and closed her eyes. 'Oh well,' she said faintly, 'show me the red-blooded girl who could refuse an offer like that.'

After an erratic few weeks during which we met, agreed to part for the sake of the child, and came together again for the sake of the sex I wanted but wasn't getting and Sara may have wanted too but also wasn't getting, our lives fell into some sort of mutually acceptable pattern. We lunched in a vegetarian restaurant once or twice a week and walked through the local stores or visited the library in the time we had left. We talked trivialities to avoid talking about our frustrations. I went back to more or less full time work in the factory, relieving Bobby of production control and dispatch. Leaving him the cutting room, the wholesale buyers, and the bloody minded quality controllers who seemed to think a factory producing three and a half thousand garments for the major stores could regularly produce three and a half thousand beautifully pressed models with never a missing button or a crooked label to be adjusted or a length of cotton to cut off.

Meanwhile those members of the assembled company who were born with balls and those who were born with breasts had their vital parts regularly chopped into mince meat by a sex starved, axe wielding, all howling, all dancing Crazy Bear.

Joan, who accidentally contrived to cook too much dinner for her and Vic every Friday evening, was responsible for my putting on a stone in weight and I managed to cut down a little on the drink. Gradually, I was reaching the stage where I could look at Margery's photograph and try to think back to the good times we shared instead of the bad times we were forced to live through. One evening I walked in on Joan sitting on my sofa with her eyes closed and holding the photograph. She opened her eyes when she heard me open the door.

'Sorry, Michael dear,' she said, quickly returning the photograph to a side table. 'I hope you don't mind. She looks so happy. I enjoy chatting to her.'

32

Not knowing if I minded or not, I shook my head and told her the frame was a gift and a bit too heavy-looking for the photograph. I kept meaning to change it for something lighter.

Joan gently ran her fingers over the moulded edge. 'You mustn't,' she said. 'Michael, you mustn't ever.'

Sarah and Julie took two more trips with me that July. One to the coast and the other to the Regent's Park Zoo where we saw the child's face glow as she gave her love to the animals and freeze when she turned back to us. It was Delia who eventually broke the impasse. My sister-in-law who just happened to be in the neighbourhood at twelve o'clock on a Wednesday and was so happy to have bumped into us. She insisted on joining us for lunch, was deeply suspicious of the soya based mince, and got herself brutally scalped by Crazy Bear before the dessert she couldn't possibly touch, darlings, puddings are so fattening. After we delivered Sara to the insurance broker for whom she worked and were on our way back to the factory, Delia said unexpectedly, 'There's nothing going on between you. Why not?'

I felt my face grow hot. 'How do you know what goes on between us?' I answered defensively. 'You're not around all the time.'

'Don't be silly darling,' she said dismissively, 'I'm not blind. You'd be looking at each other in a different way. You'd touch her when you leave and you'd be saying different things. You know perfectly well what I mean. I thought you'd be good for each other. What's wrong?'

'Nothing is wrong,' I insisted. 'We enjoy each other's company. She's trying to turn me into one of those vegetarians whose stomachs don't rumble all the time. I even drink a carrot juice three times a week. What more do you want from me?'

Delia clicked her tongue. 'Sara's an attractive young woman. Anyone can see she likes you. The question is, what more do you want?'

'I don't know what I want,' I confessed. I drove on in silence, not letting myself listen to Delia's chatter. I really didn't know what I wanted any more. It was easy to think about sex as though it existed on its own. Something you did with a stranger in a shop doorway or on the local common. Someone who dropped her knickers for a few quid and forgot what you looked like five minutes later.

But that kind of sex was no different to tossing off. I wanted the warmth and the softness and the smell of a woman in my arms. I wanted to bury my face in her hair but I didn't know how I would react to having a woman that close to me again. Responding to my love-making like Margery. Breathing like Margery. Maybe even nipping my ear between her teeth like Margery. Listening like Margery to all the stupid bad jokes I made when I got excited. I'm the new doctor, Mrs Proctor. Giving you an injection in the middle section. Face to face or belly to belly, I'm happy either way. Face to face or belly to belly. Face to face.

'Oh Jesus Christ, I was thinking as we drove through the factory gates, how much more of this can a man take?'

I drove into my parking place, drew a deep breath, and said as casually as I could, 'I really don't know what I want, Delia. It's early days yet. Do you want me to drop you here or are you coming in to see Bobby?'

Delia stayed in her seat and gave me one of her impatient looks. 'It is not early days. It's not early days at all. Why haven't you taken Sara out in the evenings?'

'That's easy,' I told her, swallowing the bait whole. 'We haven't gone out in the evenings because of her daughter Julie. She misses her father, resents her mother, and can't stand the sight of me. Sara says she's too young to leave on her own and too old for a baby sitter.' Quite suddenly I began to feel grateful to the child. The barrier she set up between Sara and me distanced the probability that I might be putting up a few barriers of my own.

'I'd like to take Sara out one evening, of course I would,' I said winningly, 'but it's Julie. It's not her fault but she makes it impossible for us to be alone together.'

'And that's the only reason?'

'Of course it's the only reason. Sara's daughter loves her father and hates me. It's only natural.'

'I suppose it is.' Delia pursed her lips and gave me a peck on the cheek before scooping up her bag and gloves. I nodded and opened the door for her.

'Even so...' she began as she got out.

'I don't want you to worry about it,' I said while I encouraged Crazy Bear to plunge a hunting knife into her back and smear the blood on his naked thighs. 'We're doing very nicely as we are.'

34

It took two weeks, four lunches, and an outing with Julie to Richmond Park for Sara to say, 'I'm sorry to hear your brother's not feeling well.'

'Isn't he?' I replied. 'He seemed all right last night. Perhaps I'll look in on him later.'

'I don't think it's anything serious. Just a minor tummy upset. The thing is, Delia offered to have Julie this evening if we'd like to have their tickets for the concert at the Fairfield Halls.'

'But what about Julie?' I asked. 'Will she mind spending the evening with Delia?'

Sara smiled up at me. 'I think she'll love it, the little minx. Your sister-in-law has promised her a hairdo at her favourite salon.'

Chapter Seven

Delia had whisked Julie away before I arrived. The evening was warm and clear. When I rang the doorbell, Sara appeared at once. Her hair had been trimmed to curl seductively behind her ears. She wore a sleeveless, high-necked white blouse tucked into the waistband of an ankle length blue velvet skirt. She smiled up at me, we kissed lightly on the lips, and when she sat beside me in the car, I touched her bare arm above the elbow and knew how much I ached for her. When the concert began we were more aware of each other than the music but as she was caught up by the swell of Beethoven's Eroica, she touched the back of my hand and said something I didn't catch. I turned to see her eyes wide with excitement and the tip of her tongue moisten her slightly parted lips and we kissed in a way we had never kissed before. I felt rather than heard her take a deep breath as she turned back to the orchestra. Her hand rested lightly on my wrist until the concert was over and when we returned to the car it felt natural to walk hand in hand.

'But my darling, the child is all tucked up and fast asleep in the spare bedroom,' Delia protested when we called to collect Julie. 'It's much too late to disturb her now. Bobby will deliver your daughter safe and sound, sassy hair and highlights included, first thing in the morning. How was your concert?'

'The concert was lovely.' Sara's voice was faint. 'Did you say sassy hair and highlights? I think I've seen the salon.'

Delia giggled. 'I managed to talk her out of most of it, darling. She's had a trim, wash and blow-dry, and the highlights. Your daughter isn't the quiet little thing you were at her age. I think I might come over with Bobby in the morning. Just to see your face when I unveil her.'

Sara glanced at me. 'You'll ring first. Before you come, I mean.'

Delia glanced at me too. 'Of course I'll ring first,' she replied.

'That was very nice,' Sara Leighton said when we reached her door and I took her in my arms and kissed her, 'but wouldn't you like to come in for a coffee?'

'No thank you,' I said politely as I followed her into the flat. 'Not for coffee.'

We stripped without speaking and lay together on the bed, my arm around the smooth warmth of her shoulders, her hair soft against my cheek, and it was like being with Margery but subtly different. I kissed Sara gently on the lips and as I felt her response, traced the curve of her breast, caressed the nipple, and ran my fingers down to the curve of her hips and thighs, at last finding the small bush of pubic hair. Touching till she moved her head restlessly and said 'Now, Michael, now.'

I closed my eyes and entered her and she was moving beneath me and with me, her sudden need as urgent as my own. With our lips, with our bodies, with our hearts, and with the weight of our broken breathing, we were one together until she shuddered, reached up to stroke my cheek, and murmur, 'Oh Michael, Michael, Michael. Please kiss me again.'

The next morning, the sunlight hit my eyes and woke me before I had a conscious thought. I was confused. In my flat, the morning sun didn't come into the bedroom. Sitting up, I looked for Margery's photograph on the bedside cabinet. It wasn't there. And of course it wasn't there. Margery lay beside me in the bed, rolled up in a tight ball and as usual, stealing all the bedclothes. I was a muddle of laughter and tears when I smacked her bare bottom and gabbled, 'Oh Meg, I've had such a horrible dream. I dreamt you died. I thought I lost you.' My shaking hands were gripped so tightly, I had to wrench them apart before I lifted the blanket and leaned across to take her in my arms and kiss her. 'Margery, oh Margery,' I was saying when Sarah Leighton opened one eye and asked what was wrong.

'Nothing,' I said as the world crashed to an end again and again and again and Crazy Bear wailed his despair. I tried to smile at Sara through the agony and said, 'Nothing's wrong. I just realised I'm in the wrong bedroom, that's all.'

'With the wrong woman?' The unspoken question hung between us waiting to be asked. Before it was, I said hastily, 'It was a bit of a shock waking up to see the sun shining through the wrong window, that's all.'

Sara's clear grey eyes regarded me a moment longer and then closed. 'I suppose it must have been,' she said dryly as Crazy Bear raised his tomahawk high and brought it down hard on her neat, curly head.

I shagged her again before we got out of bed. Pulling back the covers, I looked at a woman's soft smooth nakedness in the morning light. Savouring the round breasts, the rosy nipples, the curve of the stomach and the swell of her thighs. My erection hardened till it hurt and I couldn't wait to get inside her. To ram the meat home. To split her in two for not being Margery. With Crazy Bear capering round the room, whooping at the top of his voice and spinning his blooded axe through the air, I entered hard, my crooked fingers deep in her buttocks to hold her belly to belly, thigh to thigh, and to stop her escaping the punishment she deserved. As I throbbed and rammed and found some crazy rhythm inside her, she closed her eyes and responded, lifting herself to meet me again and again until I exploded with release and, unwilling to lose the moment, continued to hold her close until I felt the tears start and I lay gasping for air, my open mouth and tongue against her throat. Later, when she gently patted my shoulder and said she'd best get up and make us some breakfast before I got my breath back and wanted to start again, I moved away without protest.

Margery, after we'd made love and I was gently massaging whichever ear she'd chewed on during the exercise, would put on a sex show for me, rolling her hips and winking over her shoulder as she got out of bed and then, leaving the bedroom door open, she'd walk naked into the shower. When Sara got out of the bed, she slipped her dressing gown on in a totally unsexy way. Pulling it close around her, she tied the sash and walked out of the bedroom without looking back at me. After the door closed behind her, I sat on the side of the bed, searching for my clothes.

I was hurt and angry. Mostly with myself for knowing how different our love making had been the night before when Sara held me close against her breast and called me Michael three times. Whatever she was thinking the second time we had sex, for me it had been lust and had nothing to do with love. Feeling ashamed of the way I behaved, I pulled my shirt over my head, turned my underpants the right way out and stepped into them. Dragging on my trousers and finding my socks seemed to take forever because by then I knew if she couldn't be Margery, Sara Leighton could have been anybody.

I was wiping my eyes when I felt the agony of a crashing blow from Crazy Bear. He towered above me, waving his hunting knife under my nose. He screamed at me for being a stupid prick. We'd done all right, hadn't we? We got what we came for, didn't we? What the fuck did I expect from a piece of cunt? I shook my head and told him I wanted more. I didn't know what exactly but more. His eyes blazed into mine and he shouted that cunt means nothing. Cunt is supposed to mean nothing. It wasn't as though I was thinking of marrying it, was it? I shook my head again. I didn't know what I thought of doing with the cunt or the woman it was part of. My head ached and all I wanted to do was get out of there.

Sara Leighton and I laughed and told old jokes over our breakfast of scrambled eggs and toast. Both of us doing a good job of hiding the fact that we had nothing to say to one another. When I mimed patting my stomach and saying no to the last piece of toast, Sara offered me a refill of my coffee. I pushed my cup forward and as she leaned across the table to pour, her dressing gown fell open, exposing the breasts I'd cupped in my hands and kissed in the night.

'Sorry,' she said, modestly dropping her eyes and pulling the gown close around her.

'Don't be sorry,' I gabbled fatuously, 'you have beautiful breasts. You're a lovely woman and I'm very grateful to you.'

'Grateful to me?' she repeated as she reseated herself at the small kitchen table. 'I don't think I want you to be grateful to me. It makes me feel I provided a service.'

Crazy Bear cackled and I felt my face grow hot when I said, 'Oh come on, Sara. You know me better than that.'

'Do I, Michael?'

'Of course you do. You know damn well I didn't mean it that way. I'd be a prize idiot if I did. I'm grateful for your company these last few months. I'm grateful you enjoyed the concert we went to last night. I'm grateful you let me into your bed. I didn't think of it as providing a service.'

Sara shrugged and returned the coffee pot to its stand. 'Last night, I didn't think so either. When we made love it felt very special. This morning was different. It may not be your fault, Michael, but this morning I felt I could have been anybody. I felt I was acting the tart for someone I didn't know and I didn't like it.'

I put down my coffee cup. 'It was my fault,' I admitted. 'This morning I used you like a tart. Last night meant a lot more to me too.'

'Maybe it did,' Sara said, looking away, 'but I think what you did this morning may have been more honest. It seems to work better for men if they can get what they want without any emotional ties. It was all my husband wanted from having sex with me.'

I could see she was hurt and when the telephone rang, I was glad to be saved the impossibility of trying to explain about waking up and thinking she was Margery. Hearing Delia's screech of 'Darling' made me swallow my coffee at a scalding gulp and scramble to my feet.

Sara raised a hand to stop me. 'There's no hurry,' she said, replacing the receiver. 'They overslept and won't be bringing Julie for a couple of hours yet.' Her wrap had loosened again when she got up to answer the telephone and I was looking at her breasts as she came back to the table. Noticing, she smiled, shook her head warningly, and pulled the wrap close again.

'Darned thing,' she said lightly as she knotted the sash twice. 'I knew it would get me into trouble one day.'

I returned the smile and accepted another cup of coffee. 'In lieu,' I told her, 'but I really had better go in a few minutes. For one thing, I need a shave. Let me come back later. I'll buy you lunch.'

'It's Saturday. Julie will be with me.'

'That's all right. I don't mind being seen with two beautiful ladies. Besides, it'll give me the chance to admire her new hair style.'

'You may never see her new hair style. If I hate it on sight, my daughter will be wearing a turban until it grows out.'

'Get on with you,' I laughed. 'You know you can trust Delia. She has impeccable taste. She hates my wallpaper and she hates my new jacket. What time shall I pick you up?'

Sara shook her head. 'No, Michael, not today. It's too soon. You're behaving as though we're lovers and we're not. What happened between us began last night and ended this morning. I don't want either of us to feel committed. You don't have to see me again if you don't want to.'

I looked down and saw I was cradling my coffee cup in both hands like a child. 'Do you want to see me again?' I asked carefully.

'I'm not sure. It depends on what you mean by see. I enjoy our lunches. I'm greedy enough to hate the idea of going back to a cheese sandwich and a thermos flask five days a week. Sometimes it's even been bearable when we've taken Julie out.'

'And what about last night?' I prompted. 'As in sex?'

'That's what I don't know about. If it has to depend on my daughter being kept out of the way by Delia every time we feel like going to bed, I don't think so.'

'We've got a couple of hours before they get here,' I said. 'We could talk about it.'

'Tuesday,' she replied. 'Let's have lunch on Tuesday. It will be further away. We can talk about it then.'

'Right,' I said getting to my feet. Putting my hands on her shoulders, I drew her towards me for a kiss. Feeling her pull away, I dropped my hands and put them behind my back. 'Right,' I said again as I opened the door, 'Tuesday it is.'

The tall fair-haired man I passed on the stairs with a muttered apology looked vaguely familiar. I puzzled over him for the minute or two it took to get down to the street and into the car. And forgot him again when I put the car in gear and drove off. On my way home, I wondered why some people call it having a good time. Not the love-making part. Whatever my motives were, the sex had been as good as ever. It was the other half of the equation. Becoming involved. Trying to have a civilized conversation with someone you were poking like a furnace an hour or so earlier. Now that you'd found and spent the night with Sara Leighton, you didn't know if you wanted to go on poking her whenever her little girl happened to be otherwise engaged or have the good sense to run for the hills.

Well yes, you did know. So did Crazy Bear. You both enjoyed sex and, having been waiting for a good shag for a hell of a long time, you wanted to go on shagging for as long as you could get a hard on. 'But only when it's convenient, Mrs Leighton', I could say like a gentleman. 'On the odd occasions you can spare the time to drop your knickers for an old friend. In between our lunchtime shopping expeditions perhaps. Or the once a month Sundays Julie spends with her father and you turn into a nail biting, halfway up the wall neurotic who can't get her mind off what they are saying to one another and what they might be planning to hit you with next. Wouldn't that be a good time to say sod the pair of them and throw your best pair of panties over the chandelier?'

I left the car outside the garage, ran up the stairs to my flat, opened the door, stepped over the small heap of letters on the mat, and walked into the bedroom. Picking up Margery's photograph, I said, 'Hey, what do you think? I fucked another woman. In fact, I fucked her twice. Isn't that something? I don't need you any more. You're yesterday's news. Doesn't that make me a helluva fella?'

As ever, Margery smiled up at me and the smile reminded me that we always took a shower after sex, sometimes separately and at other times, on the days I had time to get excited all over again, together.

'I wish I could take you in with me this time,' I was saying to the photograph as I obediently stripped off. The water was almost hot enough to scald but I felt grubby and welcomed the shock. As I scrubbed and steam clouded round me, I somehow lost the soap. While I was on my knees scrabbling around for it with the water pounding on my head, I managed to pull down and soak the towel.

I'd fucked up with Sara Leighton, I didn't know when I was going to get another shag. I didn't know how I was going to get through the rest of my life. Forgetting the towel, I crawled out of the shower and cut my lower lip chewing on it. I could feel blood dripping down my chin and chest when I walked down the stairs into the hallway, fell against Joan and Vic's front door, and politely said to whoever opened it, 'I'm awfully sorry. I don't think I'm very well.'

Chapter Eight

I hadn't registered with a doctor since moving to the flat and I didn't know the heavily built, dark skinned man leaning over me. 'Patel,' he introduced himself, expertly buttoning me into my pyjama jacket and easing my head down on the pillow. 'There are quite a few of us about. Your neighbour found you in the hall outside. She tells me you've been looking a little off colour for some time.'

'I suppose I have,' I replied. 'I was nothing like this before my wife died. I've changed a lot since my wife died.'

He tutted soothingly, opened his case and took out a prescription pad. 'Just something to give you a good night's sleep,' he said while he scribbled. 'When did the lady pass over?'

Crazy Bear squatted on his heels in the corner of the room, his long hair loosened and his head bowed. Knowing he was praying to his ancestors, I said for his benefit as much as the doctor's, 'The lady did not pass over. The lady died. I had her cremated. I scattered her ashes. I planted a rose bush and I can't tell hers apart from all the bloody rose bushes other people planted.'

Patel gently scratched the bridge of his nose with his pen, told me the best way to avoid hyperventilation is to take a few slow deep breaths and then tell him why it troubled me to hear the words passed over instead of died.

'Because that kind of talk is pie in the sky after you die bullshit. Margery is dead. I haven't got her any more. I don't know where she is.'

'But my dear man,' Patel said as he closed his prescription pad and dropped it back in his case. 'You do know where she is. You told me the lady has gone on Holy Pilgrimage and will be known by her deeds. Her earthly remains are enshrined in living flowers and her loved one's memories.' He leaned back in his chair and smiled at me. 'It would help you to study Eastern philosophy, my friend. You would be a healthier man today.' He got to his feet and patted me on the shoulder. 'I will ask your kind neighbour Joan to get a prescription made up but I think you might sleep without it. It will do you good to sleep.'

Patel had gone and the wall lights were switched on when I woke to see an anxious looking Joan sitting beside me. 'Sorry, but I was worried about you,' she said, putting a hand on my forehead. 'Doctor Patel told me you needed to rest but you might be able to manage a little soup about now. If you think you can drink it, I'll heat it up for you.'

'I can do it myself, thanks,' I said, starting to sit up. 'I've put you to too much trouble already.'

She planted a firm hand on my chest. 'Over my dead body, you'll get up and do it yourself. Doctor Patel's strict orders are you stay in bed till further notice.'

'And did Doctor Patel leave a bedpan with his strict orders?' I asked coldly. Joan responded with a blush and a schoolgirl giggle and scrambled to her feet.

'Sorry,' she said as she disappeared into the kitchen. 'You make yourself comfortable and I'll get on with things. These clever dick doctors don't know everything.'

So tired I could hardly keep my eyes open, I sat in the kitchen to drink the soup, said 'night night' and 'thank you kindly' to Joan, went back to bed and slept till eight o'clock next morning.

My sister-in-law rang at ten. 'Darling, it's Delia. How are you? Your dragon-lady neighbour wouldn't let anyone near you last night. She telephoned to say you're laid up and your doctor wants you to rest. She said you ought to be feeling a little better this morning. Do you?'

'I think so,' I replied. 'It was nothing much really. What our dad would have called having a funny turn.'

'It didn't sound at all funny to me. Joan seemed to think you were quite ill with whatever it was. Did the doctor leave a prescription? Can I get you anything?'

'He wrote one out but if he didn't give it to Joan, I don't know what happened to it. It doesn't matter. It was only a sedative and I slept anyway. He said sleep would do me good and I think it has.'

'Can I look in for a coffee later?' Delia persisted. 'I thought we might have a chat.'

'My dragon-lady ordered me to take things easily today and besides, I think the doctor's coming back. Can we make it tomorrow?'

'Of course we can, darling. It was only about Sara. Nothing that can't wait.'

'Sara?' I repeated, memories of the encounter coming back. 'Oh yes, Sara. Do you mind telling her I can't make lunch tomorrow? You can say I've got a twenty-four hour bug of some sort. She'll understand.'

'Actually, that was it darling. She can't make it either. Her boss is away and she's been saddled with a lot of extra work. She said she'd have to cut down on meals out for a while. She'll be in touch.'

'Sounds like a brush off to me,' I said, knowing that after my performance it was more likely a bugger off and I suspected Delia knew it too. She sounded as though she was lying when she protested, 'I don't think it was meant that way, Michael. I believe Sara could get very fond of you. She told me how much she enjoyed your company the other evening.'

'I enjoyed her company too,' I lied back. 'We had a good time at the concert and afterwards.'

'Thank God for that.' Delia's voice sounded strained. 'If I thought I did anything to harm you, Michael, I'd never forgive myself.

'Right now,' I told her truthfully, 'I don't know if it harmed me or not. Going to bed with someone other than Margery had to happen some time. If I've got a problem, it's with me. Sara Leighton isn't part of it.'

After I put the phone down, I felt relieved. My aborted attempt at a love affair was over. I was off the hook and I wasn't going to be put to the test again. I grinned happily at Joan when she knocked on the door and walked into the flat with steamed fish, mashed potatoes and peas on a blue and white plate.

'You're looking better,' she said, returning the smile. 'I've brought your letters in with your dinner.'

The only letter that needed answering was from my younger son. I hadn't replied to any of his last three. Before I could change my mind, I scribbled, 'Dear Dicky, when you were at school you took an interest in local history. Did you know Anne Boleyn lived near here? If you can come down for the weekend, it'll give me the opportunity to show you where her horse kicked up a stone and sprung a well and drowned half the population of Carshalton according to my neighbour Joan who believes every word she's told, even by me.

You can doss down on the couch or sleep over at Bobby and Delia's and have your aunt make a fuss of you.' I left the letter on the windowsill for posting and came back to telephone his brother.

'Dad,' George said, sounding more concerned than I expected. 'How are you? Aunty Delia said you're not too well and not to bother you for a day or two.'

'I bet she also told you not to call her Aunty Delia.'

George laughed a little ruefully. 'Now that you mention it, she keeps telling me not to call her Aunty Delia and I keep getting one of her dirty looks for forgetting. Are you really feeling better, Dad? If there's anything you want I can come over this evening.'

'Company,' I said. 'There's nothing I need but I wouldn't say no to a little company.'

'I'll be with you at half past six. Remember what you used to say when you rang home from the factory?'

'See you soon. Put the kettle on?'

'That's it Dad. See you soon. Put the kettle on.'

'I'm not stopping you seeing your girl friend?'

'Not tonight, Dad. I'll see you later on.'

I put the phone down. My palms were wet, my hands were shaking, Crazy Bear was muttering something about jelly belly yelly, and I was desperate for a drink. I'd written a few words to one son, spoken to the other for a minute and a half, and I had to have a drink because they were my kids and I didn't know what to say to them. I half filled a whisky tumbler, took it to the hall mirror, and toasted the pathetic sod with the white, shit-scared face looking back at me.

'That wasn't so hard, was it?' I asked the face. 'It's only George and Dicky. They're your sons. Once upon a time you used to tell them stories. Once upon a time you used to smack their little bums. You know what you have to say to George and Dicky. 'I killed your mother. I was so busy dragging her from pillar to post looking for miracle cures I wouldn't give her the chance to rest. I wouldn't let her die in peace. I wouldn't even let myself believe she was dying till it was too late.'

I poured myself another drink, imagined sitting the boys side by side on the couch and telling them how sorry I was for killing Margery. I'd wanted to say I was sorry for a long time but I didn't know how. I didn't know anything except I hated myself for letting it happen and it was only natural that they should hate me too. And when I looked at it, my glass was empty and so was the bottle.

I opened a fresh bottle and poured a double and was halfway through it before I knew I wouldn't say any of those things. Crazy Bear knew it, too. He sat on the couch spinning his tomahawk boomerang fashion and deftly catching it by the haft when it rounded the room and came back to his hand. When I upended my fourth tumbler and somehow made it back to face the figure in the mirror, he threw the tomahawk hard at me. I pressed back against the wall to see it hover an inch from my chest before it swung away and returned to his hand.

'You heap big shit scared yelly belly cowardly custard,' the chief said again, a note of gloomy satisfaction in his voice.

George has no sense of time. Margery used to complain about it all the time. I used to think he did it deliberately, just to irritate me. And he succeeded. Knowing I'd be waiting at half past six with a plate of sandwiches and a pot of tea, he turned up an hour later. No apologies, that would be too much to hope for. After a mutter of 'Hi, Dad', he flopped on the couch and stared at the wallpaper. Anything rather than meet my eyes. I ostentatiously made a fresh pot of tea, poured him a cup, and stepping across his legs to hand it to him, had to resist the urge to kick his ankle. I'd forgotten he had such long legs and the awkward way they stuck out irritated me. It's not that I didn't know he's a head and a half taller than me, it just kept slipping my mind that it's all in the legs. His jeans were torn, his shoes were filthy, he made noises drinking his tea, and he wiped his mouth with the back of his hand. His hair needed cutting. His shirt was crumpled and unbuttoned to halfway down his chest.

Not that I was going to say a word. It was none of my business if I had a son who walked round looking like a tramp. If I had a pound for every time I told him that ninety per cent of what people see of him are the clothes on his back, I'd be a rich man by now. If the idgit didn't know better than to walk about in filthy shoes and dandruff on his collar, it was his mouldy cheese. He knows his mother wouldn't like it. He knows I don't like it. The truth is, I hate it. His mother and I said it all in the past. Water off a duck's back. I should have kept my mouth shut then and I was bloody sure of keeping it shut now. I hadn't brought him up to the flat to have a row.

'Donna and I are thinking of getting married in August,' he said, handing me his cup for a refill.

'That's nice,' I replied while I poured his tea and gave myself another whisky. 'It'll give you time to clean your shoes and get your hair cut.'

George flushed, looked at his shoes, and then grinned up at me. 'You don't change, do you? I just told you I'm getting married. If Mum was here, she'd say how marvellous, how soon can you bring the girl and her parents round for dinner. And you'd still be telling me to get my hair cut and clean my shoes before you meet them.'

'If your mother was here, I wouldn't be living in this shit hole,' I said, feeling my hands start to shake. 'If your mother was here, I wouldn't be ill. If your mother was here...' George was shaking his head and cupping his ear but I ignored him and carried on, 'if your mother was here, I wouldn't have taken Delia's friend Sara Leighton to her flat last night and shagged her rotten.'

'Dad,' George said patiently, 'you are pissed as a newt and I don't know what you're going on about. Why don't you lie down for an hour? You're not making any sense.'

'I'm making perfect sense,' I told him through the bottom of my glass. 'If you'd only stop yakking and listen to me.'

George shook his head again and looked at his wristwatch. 'Listen, Dad, as soon as you feel better, Donna's mum and dad would like you over for a meal. Can I fix it for one evening next week?'

'I was talking about your mother, George.'

'I know you were, Dad, but what's there to say? Mum's not here any more. We are and we have to go on living. I'll give you a ring tomorrow.'

'You're not going already? You only just got here.'

George stood up and stretched, his fingers brushing the ceiling. 'I've got to go now, I'm sorry. Let me arrange with Donna's mum about the dinner. She's their only daughter and they want to talk to you about the wedding. They want to know if we've got any pretty little girls tucked up our sleeves who want to be bridesmaids and which of our relatives and friends we'd like to invite. You know the sort of thing.'

'Your mother would have been a lot better at it than I will.'

'Oh no she wouldn't. You were always the organizer. And you always said so.' He walked to the door and as he passed, I felt his hand press my shoulder.

'If your mother was here...' I began but he was gone.

'If your mother was here,' I told the door he closed behind him, 'she and Delia would have a list of bridesmaids and wedding guests as long as your arm in five minutes and would change their minds fifty times in the next ten.'

I topped up my glass and took it into the bedroom. 'You're supposed to look out for me at times like these,' I told Margery, 'so where the hell are you? Your son's getting married. The bride's parents want to know about bridesmaids and wedding guests from our side. What the bloody hell do I know about bridesmaids? I bet Delia knows all about it by now. She'll be licking her chops and making plans. You just wait and see what she does to screw it up without you here to stop her. She's the one who ought to be meeting George's future in-laws, not me.' Margery smiled at me out of the photograph and said nothing.

Dissatisfied, I walked into the kitchen and picked up the telephone. 'I suppose you and Delia know all about George's wedding by now,' I said accusingly.

Bobby laughed. 'Do we know? Delia's already working out how much her wedding outfit is going to cost me. Hang on, she wants to talk to you.'

'No Bobby,' I said, 'not now. It's almost half past seven. Joan must be on her way up with my dinner and I haven't got time for one of Delia's long conversations.'

'Don't be ridiculous, darling,' Delia purred. 'It'll only take a moment to tell you about my wonderful idea. Bobby loves it.'

'Does he?' I asked suspiciously. 'What wonderful idea?'

'Little Julie, darling. She's so sweet. She'll make a beautiful bridesmaid.'

'Little Julie as in Sara Leighton's little Julie?' The woman had to be mad. I was just beginning to get myself together and she wanted to start the Sara nonsense all over again. She was mad. I'd always known it. Crazy Bear had told her she was sick in the head a thousand times.

'You've got to be mad…' I began when she interrupted me with, 'I've already telephoned Sara. She's thrilled to bits. She says the child can't wait.'

'Delia,' I yelped as the door opened and Joan walked in carrying a tray.

'Must go, darling. Give it a think and ring me in the morning.'

'Hey Mr Brent,' Joan said while she put the tray on the table, 'you know you're not supposed to let yourself get excited. I could hear you half way up the stairs.'

'Who wouldn't get excited,' I snarled. 'My son's getting married and my bloody sister-in-law wants to take the whole thing over.'

Joan didn't look in the least surprised. 'Well of course she does,' she said comfortingly. 'What woman wouldn't? Sit down. Your dinner's getting cold.'

I plonked myself down in a chair. 'She even wants to start picking the bridesmaids.'

'Sara Leighton's little girl, I suppose.'

I gave her a short nod. 'That's right, Julie. Ridiculous, isn't it?'

'Oh yes,' Joan agreed while she handed me a knife and fork. 'Quite ridiculous.'

'And what's so blooming funny?' I wanted to know, looking her straight in the eye and daring her to laugh. She waited until she got through the door.

Chapter Nine

I liked the look of George's future father-in-law the moment I set eyes on him. He was a big, no nonsense, straight from the shoulder kind of man with a square jaw and an air of self confidence I normally associated only with Crazy Bear. I was wondering how he would look wearing a feathered headdress and sitting on the back of a horse when he gave me a firm shake of the hand, introduced himself as Ted, acknowledged me as Michael, and led the way into a small annex set out like a bar.

Waving at the neat row of bottles, he told me in his no nonsense way to take a pew and tell him what I was drinking.

I perched on one of the shiny leatherette stools and said, 'Well Ted, I don't drink a lot these days but I'll have a small whisky with you, just to celebrate the occasion.'

'Good man,' he said, handing me a half-full tumbler of whisky and pouring himself a beer. 'Get that inside you and we'll have a quiet man to man before my Clara dishes up our spot of supper.'

'Thank you, Ted,' I said gratefully. 'Thank you very much.' I swallowed a little of the whisky and admired the way he sat in a legs apart, 'master of all I survey' manner. Ted had the look of a man who could cope with life's little problems. Like his Clara being dead and not knowing where to go for a bit of the other without feeling so guilty you make yourself ill for three weeks. Not that his Clara showed any sign of dying. Not of hunger anyway. I'd shaken hands with the little butterball when she let me into their plushy front hall and called Ted in from the garden. Returning her smile, I wondered if George saw her as a dreadful warning of what his Donna might become one day. It probably hadn't crossed his mind. If I thought it would do any good, I'd have tried to warn him off but he'd only resent it. He was another Margery. Took his time making his mind up about people but once he had, there was no shifting him. He was loyal and so was young Dicky. It had been stupid to feel afraid of them. Or of Delia and her tricks. If I had any sense, I'd be more like good old Ted here. Ted, who was on his feet and saying something I hadn't quite caught the drift of.

'Sorry Ted?'

'I was saying your son is a credit to you but you've finished your drink. Let me give you another.'

I held out my glass.

'Now listen, Michael,' he went on as he tipped the bottle, 'I'm a blunt man and since my girl is marrying your son, I hope you won't mind a bit of straight talking. How are you fixed for money?'

I raised my eyebrows. 'Er, why do you want to know that, Ted?'

'Well, old man, it's like this. Donna's our only daughter and I want to do the job one hundred per cent. I'm not going to have any spoiling the ship for a ha'porth of tar on this wedding. The thing is, Michael, I'm told it's usual for the bridegroom's side to pick up the tab for some of the expenses. Cars and flowers. Booze and some small gifts for the bridesmaids. That sort of thing. Now, I'm not saying this to embarrass you. All I want is a clear understanding from the start. If you want to, Michael, now's the time to tell me you're a bit strapped for cash and you don't think you can manage to cover the cost. If you do, I'll take the whole thing off your hands and we won't say another word about it. I can't make it plainer than that, can I?'

I shook my head. 'No you can't make it any clearer and it's very kind of you to think of it, Ted. As it happens, the factory is doing pretty well and there's quite a bit left over from the sale of my house. I'll be glad to pay my share of the expenses.'

'Oh good,' Ted said. 'That's very good. I'm glad it won't break the bank.'

He sounded disappointed and I added hastily, 'But I'd be more than grateful if you and Clara would take the arrangements off my hands and let me have the bill. I don't mind paying my whack but I wouldn't be the least bit of use at making arrangements.'

'Of course we'll see to the arrangements.' Ted said, clapping me warmly on the shoulder. 'It's the very least we can do. I can imagine what it must be like to be a man on his own.'

Clara had changed her clothes when she put her head into Ted's den and said, 'Come on you two boys, that's enough talking for one evening. Dinner is served.' She was wearing an orange and black blouse that showed far too much cleavage for a short fat woman and a full length black skirt draped her ample hips. Filling my plate first for each course, she served an avocado and prawn starter, followed by chops, each of which wore a miniature chef's hat on its bony end.

She leaned her warm powdered bosoms on my shoulder while she piled glossy baked potatoes, carrots and peas on my plate. Rightly or wrongly, I copied Ted by picking up my chop and gnawing it as though I hadn't eaten in a week. The sweet was a helping of hot limp apple pie, generously smothered in cream.

'Thank you, that looks delicious,' I said at each serving. Clara twittered gratefully and told me I really ought to have another potato. Anyone could see I was much too thin for a man of my height. She was sure I wouldn't mind her saying she thought I wasn't looking after myself properly. Men who lived on their own never did look after themselves properly. They had no idea of how to run a home, the poor dears. That was the real tragedy of a man losing his wife and having to cope with being the one left behind. Not that I wasn't coping marvellously, she was quite sure I was. She knew only too well that if she died in tragic circumstances like my poor wife died, her darling Ted would go completely to pieces. Ted leaned across the table and patted the back of her dimpled hand before he said, 'But you're not going to die, are you Mummykins. You know your Daddykins couldn't live without you.'

I persuaded myself it was the greasy baked potatoes and the cream smothered apple tart that made me want to vomit over the pair of them. For George's sake, I held the maddened Crazy Bear in check. Before I could get away, Clara stood on tiptoe to kiss my cheek and good old Ted gave me another manly shake of the hand.

'Don't you dare be a stranger now you've found us,' said Clara, wagging a finger in my face. 'You're part of our family now.'

'She took them golden words right out of my mouth,' said Ted, giving my hand another manly squeeze before slapping my back.

The grin I thought I'd plastered permanently to my face was swallowed by a snarl when I got into the car and slammed the door behind me. Racing the engine, I let Crazy Bear run wild until Clara and good old Ted's faces were gap toothed bloody wrecks and their bloated and grotesquely distorted bodies were tied to stakes and lit by the flames that destroyed them. I could smell burning hair and flesh and taste their salty blood on my lips when Ted tapped on the car window and I almost jumped three feet in the air.

Peering in at me, he bellowed, 'Lights, old man. Don't forget to switch on your lights. Clara says safe journey home.' I nodded and snapped the lights on.

'I won't forget the lights,' I growled as I drove past his waving hand. 'Or your livers. You wait, you mother-fucking bastard. Me and Crazy Bear will have your guts for garters. You and your fat sow can live till after my son's wedding. Then you die ten thousand deaths. Each!'

I risked my neck by driving home too fast, left the car more or less outside the garage, and ran up the stairs to get in the flat and sick up Mummykins and Daddykins and all their filthy foodykins, only Dicky was there. In the sitting room, standing between me and the bog.

'Your neighbour Joan let me in, Dad. I was watching you drive into the car park and you left your lights on. If you'd like to give me the keys, I'll nip down and turn them off before your battery goes flat.'

'Oh did I?' I said, starting to search through my pockets. 'I'm always doing something stupid these days. I must be getting old.' The keys weren't to be found. I fumbled through my pockets again, couldn't find them, and got angry all over again.

'Look,' I shouted. 'Stop waving your fucking hands under my nose and stop going on about the fucking lights. I don't know why you silly bastards can't make your minds up. Ted wants the lights on, you want the lights off. What's the matter with the two of you?'

'I expect you left the key in the ignition,' Dicky said patiently. 'I'll go down and check. Why don't you sit down? I'll make you a cup of coffee when I get back.'

Dicky shouldn't have been patient and he shouldn't have tried to humour me. I'd had a terrible time with good old Ted and his fat little Clara. I was desperate for a drink. I'd no idea what I'd done with the car keys. He was standing too close to me. So I punched him in the mouth as hard as I could and fell back on the couch looking up at him.

'You pathetic old sod,' my son Dicky said, not touching the thread of blood that had began to run down his chin. 'Why didn't you die instead? Mum was worth ten of you.'

I watched him go through the door and close it quietly behind him. Then I stretched out on the couch and sobbed myself to sleep like a baby.

The next morning, he rang at eight. 'I'm at Aunty Delia's, Dad, and I've got your car keys. Can I come in and see you or would you rather I put them through the letterbox?

'Of course I want you to come in and see me,' I told him. 'I'm only sorry I'm not your mother.'

'It was said in the heat of the moment, Dad. You know I didn't mean it. Forget it ever happened and I'll see you after breakfast.'

Chapter Ten

Sleeping on the old couch used to be easy. If for any reason, Margery was restless, angry with me, or as happened later, was ill, that's where I spent my nights, wrapped in a torn old comfort blanket. Sometimes I woke with a kink in my spine or an ear flattened into temporary deafness but on the whole, I woke refreshed after an undisturbed sleep. But not this time. When I crawled off the couch, my head was splitting, my eyes were sore, my throat was dry, and I felt like shit. With a hand against the wall for support, I made it into the bedroom, collapsed on the bed, and picked up Margery's photograph.

'Dicky told me to forget it happened,' I told her. 'I'm supposed to let him come up here and forget he said I should have died instead of you. The truth is he was right. If it was you waiting for him, he'd walk in and you'd be cuddled and comforted by your big strong handsome son who is the bloody spitting image of you. Do you think it was him I hit last night? I don't. I think I hit you. Do you know what I went through last night with Daddykins and Mummykins who know what it's like to be a man on his own? Do you know the last time I touched Sara Leighton, I was ill for three weeks? Christ, what's the matter with everybody round here? Now the sodding doorbell's ringing and I haven't even had a cup of coffee yet.'

I hadn't had a shower either. Or a shave. Or combed my hair or cleaned my teeth. I hadn't even taken off the crumpled suit I'd slept in. I could only imagine what I must have looked and smelt like when I dragged my clothes into some semblance of order and opened the door to Sara Leighton.

'You really don't look well,' she said as if I didn't know about the dark bags under my eyes. 'When you hear these things from Delia, you never know if she's telling the truth or exaggerating. Can I come in? I need to talk to you.'

'I thought you were my boy Dicky,' I said stupidly as I stepped to one side. 'I wouldn't have come to the door like this if I'd known it was you.'

'Thank you, but it really doesn't matter. I shouldn't have disturbed you so early.' She gave me a brief smile. 'I've taken the day off. Why don't you have a shower and put on some fresh clothes. I can wait. Would you like me to make some coffee?'

'Now that sounds like the best offer I've had all day,' I said, doing my best to return the smile.

I hadn't heard the doorbell ring again from the bathroom and it came as a shock to see Dicky sitting on the kitchen table chatting to Sara. His face had a slight bruise on one side and his lower lip was swollen.

'Hi Dad,' he said, getting off the table and grinning at me. 'Here are your car keys. You left the car door open and I walked into it.'

'You didn't damage the paintwork?'

He laughed. 'Only my own. I've introduced myself to Mrs Leighton as your accident-prone younger son and just to make me feel better, she's willing to swear on the Bible that she's as clumsy as I am. Can I get you some breakfast?'

'A piece of toast would be nice,' I replied. 'I'm sorry about the car door, Dicky. I don't know what I was thinking of. It was a stupid thing to do.'

He touched me on the shoulder and turned back to the grill. 'Cheese on top? Aunty Delia gave us welsh rabbit this morning. She said it was in my honour.'

'Aunty Delia?' Sara repeated slowly. 'I must remember that. I bet she loves being called Aunty Delia.'

'No, not really,' said Dicky. 'She said she takes it from me because I'm the baby of the family. She told me to get you some grapes, dad, but I forgot. Would you like me to go down and get them now?'

'You dare bring me grapes,' I mumbled through a mouthful of toast. 'On the other hand, Mrs Leighton did come up for a chat. If you can spare an hour, maybe you'd take the car to the car wash and then get it filled up for me?' Dicky looked from Sara to me and back again.

'I don't mean to drive you out,' she told him apologetically, 'I can come back later.'

'It's no problem,' Dicky said, retrieving the car keys and smiling at her. 'It was nice meeting you. If you're not here when I get back, I hope I see you again.'

'I hope so too,' Sara replied, returning his smile.'

Together, we listened to him clatter down the stairs, shout hello to Joan and Vic as he passed them, and then bang through the outside door, making it squeal its usual protest as it swung back and forth two or three times. In the silence that followed, I glanced surreptitiously at my one night stand lover and found myself meeting her eyes.

'Alone at last,' I ventured.

She ignored the remark and said, 'Your Dicky is a very nice young man. You must be proud of him.'

'Proud?' I repeated. 'Well yes, I suppose I am when I think about it. He'll be George's best man when he marries.'

'That's nice.' She hesitated for a moment and then said, 'It's George's wedding I came to see you about. I'm embarrassed.'

'You mean about Julie being a bridesmaid?'

She nodded. 'There are times I could cheerfully kill your sister-in-law but now she's suggested it, Julie is so thrilled. Michael, she's had a rotten time lately and I couldn't bear to disappoint her again. I know things have gone wrong between us and after the wedding you needn't see me again; but I'd be so grateful...'

'Whoa back,' I interrupted. 'What's there to be grateful for? You've known Delia for years and you're a friend of the family. Why shouldn't I ask Julie to be one of Donna's bridesmaids? She's a beautiful little girl. Why did you say things have gone wrong between us?'

'Please, Michael, let's face it. I'm fond of you but I'm just getting over a bad marriage. I'm not ready for a heavy relationship. If I were, things might be different but there's no going back. We spent the night together once and if we go on meeting, we will again. Sooner or later, we'll find ourselves caught up in some hole in the corner affair that wouldn't be right for either of us.'

To keep my hands occupied, I poured myself a coffee I didn't want to drink and looked at her. She was wearing the brown linen suit she had on when we first met in Croydon. Her blouse looked crisp, neat, and uncrushable. Sitting erect on one of my straight backed kitchen chairs, her knees together, ankles neatly crossed, she looked cool and inviolable, this woman who was telling me she wasn't ready for an affair. I'd seen her smile and take her clothes off. I'd held her naked in my arms. I kissed her hair, her eyelids, and her lips. I cupped her breasts in my hands. When we made love she

58

touched my face and said Michael oh Michael oh Michael. Looking at her and remembering our night together was doing things to my body. I wondered if I could get away with taking her by the hand and leading her gently into the bedroom.

'Just this once,' I could say as I stroked the lightly veined inside of her wrist. 'Let me make it right this time. With no strings attached. You don't have to see me again if you don't want to. The bedroom is just over here. Over here..' Suddenly my mouth felt dry and I swallowed some cold coffee.

'I've got lost somewhere,' I confessed, putting the cup between us and keeping my fingers crooked round the handle. 'What were we talking about?'

'Nothing in particular,' she replied before I could reach forward to touch her fingertips. 'I was going to tell you about my husband. He came to see me last week.'

I let go of the cup and dropped my hand in my lap. 'Your husband?'

'Paul the ex. He once saw you leave my flat and immediately decided that you were the reason our marriage broke down. When he called, I tried to tell him I met you for the first time after the divorce but he wouldn't listen. He just went on and on in that flat voice of his saying he found me out at last, he always knew he would. He called me a cheap whore and said I wasn't fit to be in charge of any child, let alone his only daughter. Then Julie started to cry and hid in her bedroom while he rushed away. I'm so sorry, Michael.'

'Tallish man with fair hair?' I asked. She nodded and I went on, 'I saw him on the stairs outside your flat. Julie has his colouring. What makes him think I'm responsible for your divorce? Was it because of another man?'

'No it was not. I was very young when we married. Apart from Paul, I didn't know any men Besides, I was in love with him or I thought I was, and it wasn't long before I had Julie to bring up. I'm sorry Michael, I really don't want to talk about this. Paul treated me very badly and because he has always refused to accept that he is the only reason I took his daughter away, he's fastened on you.'

'Meaning what exactly?'

'Meaning he's coming here to have it out with you. He followed you home and he rang this morning to tell me that he's coming here.'

I surprised myself by laughing. 'What do you expect me to do? Take boxing lessons?'

Sara didn't return my smile as she got to her feet and said, 'Honestly, Michael, the last thing you need is me and my problems, especially when you've been ill. If he comes, don't let him in. If he makes a nuisance of himself, tell him you're sending for the police. I think we'd best forget about Julie being one of Donna's bridesmaids. We'd best forget about us. I'm no good for you. I'm no good for anyone.' She was crying and almost as though I hadn't planned it, I took her in my arms, kissed her forehead, and gently led her to the bedroom. 'Oh Michael,' she said, touching my cheek as we walked through the door and closed it behind us. 'Oh Michael.'

Paul Leighton called on me that evening and for no reason I could put a finger on, I wouldn't have been afraid of ten of him. 'I know who you are,' I told him as I opened the door. 'Come in and sit down.' He followed me into the sitting room and stood irresolutely by the door.

'I – I'll stand if you don't mind,' he said hesitantly.

'But I do mind,' I told him, making my voice sharp and aggressive. 'If you want to speak to me, you can sit down and have a drink. Otherwise, you can get out.'

'No spirits. I – I'll have a soft drink, please.' He took the orange juice from me and perched uncomfortably on the edge of a chair facing the bedroom I'd made love to his wife in a few hours earlier. The thought tickled me and I began to act like Crazy Bear, neatly parting his hair with my spinning tomahawk.

'I'm not going to beat about the bush,' I said as I settled on the couch. 'I know your ex-wife. I've known her since I moved into this place and my sister-in-law introduced us at my flat warming. I like her. We've lunched together a few times and we've taken Julie out once or twice. Whatever you may think, I did not know Sara while you were married and I had nothing to do with your divorce. If that's what you came to find out, now you know it. So you can drink your drink and bugger off. After the things I've heard about you and the way you behaved towards your ex-wife, you're not welcome here.'

The moment he raised his head and looked at me, I knew I'd gone too far.

Carefully setting his untouched orange juice on the table between us, he said tonelessly, 'I want you to know I am fighting for my life.

I don't know what I have to do to make you understand the situation. This time last year, I was a happily married man with a wife and a daughter. Now, through no fault of my own, I have nothing. You talk as though it doesn't matter what you do to hurt me but it does. You are stealing my wife and daughter and destroying me. I can't work. I can't sleep. I want Sara and Julie back. They are the purpose of my life. They are what I worked for and built a home for. You're telling me to bugger off because you don't want me here. Where would you like me to bugger off to? Where do you want me to go?'

He picked up his juice, took a sip, and without waiting for an answer, went on, 'I don't know Sara any more. I don't know what she wants from me. I said I was sorry I lost my temper. I was working under a lot of pressure. I got angry and I know I behaved badly. I begged her to stop the divorce proceedings. I promised to change. I can change and I want her to change her mind about me. I want her to bring Julie home. I can't go on living like this.' He stopped abruptly and rubbed a hand over his eyes before slumping back in his chair. He looked exhausted and quite suddenly my mood changed.

Feeling desperately sorry for the man, I cleared my throat and said, almost apologetically, 'A long time ago, my late wife left me. She came back with the boys in the end but it was hard going while it lasted.'

'Then you know what you're doing to me,' he muttered. 'How can you go on with it when you know how it feels to be left alone?'

Which was the kind of question I asked myself when I was in the Falklands. How do you go on killing people when you know they're made of flesh and blood? Aloud, I said, 'Paul, I was rough on you when you first came in and I'm sorry. The plain truth is, I didn't know what to expect. Sara hasn't told me why she and Julie left you and I haven't asked her for a reason. Are you honestly telling me there's a chance of reconciliation if I'm not in the picture?'

'If there's no other man involved, I know we can get together again,' he said convincingly, 'and next time it will be better for all of us.'

After we shook hands at the door and said our good-byes, I telephoned Sara. 'He spoke quite reasonably,' I told her. 'He said how desperately sorry he was for what he did wrong. He knows his suspicions ruined the marriage for you. He told me he tried to apologise but you refused to listen to him.' Uncomfortably aware that she wasn't answering, I ploughed on. 'He said he wants to change. Given the chance he will change. He said he told you he would change before the divorce but you wouldn't listen to him then, either. He looked so down, I didn't know what to think.'

'You didn't know what to think?' Sara repeated. 'How many times do you imagine he told me he would change? How many times do you think he begged me not to go before I finally walked out and took Julie with me? He would change until he had a bad day at the office and couldn't wait to come home and take it out on me.'

'Oh come on Sara,' I said. 'I could get home after a rough day and spend the next hour yelling if my dinner wasn't on the table or the kids hadn't put their toys away. I was just blowing off steam. Margery understood that.'

Sara's voice sounded strained when she asked if Margery would have understood me waiting for food to be put in front of me and then throwing the plate in her face. Or if she would have understood being knocked to the kitchen floor and having me kick her in the stomach. They weren't questions and she put the phone down before I could think of an answer. Not that there was anything to say except that Margery would have landed me one with a brick if I ever laid a finger on her. Not that I could. You don't hurt the people you love. Except by going away with the children. Or by dying, which is another kind of going away. The thought of Sara lying on the kitchen floor and being kicked in the stomach brought bile up in my throat and I poured myself a drink. She thought I betrayed her by taking her husband's side in a situation I knew nothing about and she was right. I didn't know if Paul was particularly clever or I had been stupid but he'd got what he wanted from me. I went to bed cuddling my whisky bottle, knowing it was very unlikely I'd be hearing from Sara Leighton again.

Delia, of course, couldn't wait to tear into me. 'Michael Brent,' she snarled when she telephoned the next morning. 'You are a bloody fool. For Julie's sake, Sara put up with a hell of a lot more than she'd ever tell you before she left. You let yourself be taken in by a lying vicious swine I would have murdered if he ever came near me.'

'Or bitten his head off,' I couldn't help suggesting.

62

'It's not a joke,' she snapped angrily. 'Since when did wife beating become a joke?'

'Oh come on, Delia,' I said, 'you know me better than that. I'm sorry.'

'It's not me you have to apologise to, it's Sara. If I hadn't managed to make her see sense, Julie wouldn't have been the bridesmaid after all.'

I hesitated. 'You made Sara see sense?'

'Of course I did,' said my sister-in-law. 'I told her what an idiot like you chooses to think isn't worth upsetting the child over. You'd better apologise to Sara now.'

'Delia,' I replied, 'I was wrong and of course, I'll apologise. But you don't know the man. What he said to me was very persuasive.'

'Being persuasive is his stock in trade, Michael darling. I saw him put on his act during the divorce proceedings. The truth is, he is a sadistic, bullying swine who would hurt anyone he's not afraid of.'

'All right,' I said, 'all right. I've got the picture and I was a fool to be taken in. Besides, Julie's a nice child and I'd like her to be one of Donna's bridesmaids. If you stop beating me over the head with this and put your phone down, I'll telephone Sara now.'

'She'll be on her way to work. Why don't you stop by her office later on and see if she'll have lunch with you?'

'I'll be in our warehouse all morning,' I hedged. 'I've got to get a docket of coats and suits out. I'll get away if I can.'

'You have to,' Delia ordered.

At ten minutes to one, I tapped on Sara's office window and when she looked up, mimed putting a forkful of pasta in my mouth. After a moment or two's hesitation, she nodded and stood up to put on her coat. We walked without speaking and a little apart to the restaurant. Inside, the waitress smiled at us and said, 'Hi there, how are you two these days? The usual?'

'We're fine, thanks,' I replied while I looped Sara's coat on to a rack. 'A garlic bread starter and we'll both have tagliatelli and black coffee, please.'

While we waited for the meal, we lapsed into an uncomfortable silence, Sara looking down at the paper napkin she was pleating and unpleating between her fingers, me trying to block the thought of her being knocked down and kicked in the stomach by the mild mannered Paul who drank a glass of orange juice in my flat and convinced me that I alone stood in the way of their reconciliation. At last I reached forward and covered her hand with my own.

'Sara,' I said, 'you must know I'd no idea of how your husband behaved towards you when I telephoned. He made it sound as though you had a misunderstanding. I'm truly sorry.'

Her hand lay passively beneath mine and she didn't look up when she spoke. 'The first time was when Julie was a few weeks old. I fed her and tried to put her down but she wouldn't settle and I had to pick her up again. Paul was watching a quiz show on television and he punched me for disturbing his concentration. He went on hitting and humiliating me for another eight years before I finally left him and sued for divorce. There was medical evidence of his brutality. Photographs were shown in court and my doctor was called to give evidence. Paul said I was clumsy and I bruised easily. I only needed to walk into a table or the door to raise a bruise on my arm or my leg. He admitted that he might have pushed me once or twice. He had a bit of a temper, he told the divorce judge. What man didn't lose his rag now and again? Especially when he had to watch me fussing and nagging over the child when she'd have been far better left alone. My feeble attempt at being a competent mother would have driven a saint mad and he was certainly no saint. Oh no Michael, you don't have to tell me how plausible he can be. He almost talked the judge into giving him custody of Julie.'

'Does he love her that much?' I asked.

'Paul only loves himself. It was another way of hurting me or getting me back. He told the judge he loves me and needs me but he doesn't. I don't know why he wouldn't let me go. The doctor suggested that he was a bully who had found a victim and didn't want to release her.'

'I suppose so,' I said lamely as the food was put in front of us. We began to eat in silence, each of us busy with our own thoughts. I knew about bullies. I knew about them from my schooldays. At night, I screwed myself into my bed and through my tears watched Crazy Bear slaughter them by the dozen. Staking them out, their fat bloated bodies smeared with wild honey, their screams echoing through my bedroom while soldier ants ate them alive. Or, his strong bony face streaked with war paint, he trotted his bare back pony, letting them run before him until they were sobbing for breath. One by one he cut them down, or allowed them to hope a little longer as he urged them forward to be trampled to death beneath the hooves of stampeding buffalo. Oh yes, I knew about bullies. I knew how much I hated them. And how much I hated Paul Leighton.

'Is there something wrong with the food, Michael?' Sara asked. 'I've told you that you don't have to eat vegetarian food just because I do.'

Surprised, I looked down at my almost untouched plate and picked up my knife and fork. 'No, it's fine. You've given me a lot to think about, that's all.'

I put the knife and fork down again. 'Look, what I said on the telephone. It's not going to stop you coming to the wedding is it?'

'Of course I'll be there. I wouldn't miss the chance of seeing my daughter as a bridesmaid. For all I know, it might be the only time she's asked.'

'The reception too,' I persisted. 'I don't want to be on my own at the reception.'

'You won't be on your own. Your whole family will be with you.'

'But I want you to be there too, Sara. You don't know what good old Ted and Clara are like. I need you to be there.'

'I'll come if you want but don't need me, Michael. I like you very much but I never want to be needed again. I've got a good job and I'm independent. Other than that, I just want to get on with the job of raising my daughter.'

'As friends?' I asked. 'We all need friends. Ask Max Bygraves.'

'That's hands,' said Sara. 'Eat your lunch and you'd better see to it I get a vegetarian meal at the reception.'

'You and me both,' I said, grinning at her like an idiot.

Chapter Eleven

I woke in the middle of a dream, the back of my pyjama jacket soaked with sweat. At last I had turned on the big boys. Leaping at them, I punched one on the nose to make his eyes water and blind him while I swung my school satchel at the other, sending him sprawling in the road, his fat red legs scratched and bloodied by the buckles on my satchel straps while his cap disappeared beneath a passing bus. Turning fast and low, I saw the first boy raise his hands and dropped him with a clinically accurate left to the pit of his stomach and, as he folded, a hard right to the point of the jaw.

'Stop it,' the boy whose face had become Paul Leighton's screamed through his tears, 'I've had enough. Please don't hit me any more.'

'You see? I can do it on my own. I don't need you dancing round me all the fucking time,' I was yelling at Crazy Bear when something hit the back of my head, making me bite my tongue. With Paul screeching and the pain of the blow reverberating somewhere behind my ears, I sat up in bed and heard someone rapping loudly on the front door.

'Michael, it's Vic,' Joan was calling. 'He's ill. Please come and help me.'

'What's up...' I began, putting a hand to my head where I'd thrown myself backwards to butt the headboard. Wondering if I was still dreaming, I called again, 'Joan, it's all right, I heard you. I'll be with you in a couple of shakes.'

Vic was pale, short of breath, and obviously in pain when Joan and I wrapped him in a blanket, led him slowly and gently down the stairs, and helped him into the car. It was getting on for four in the morning and while we drove to the hospital Joan told me how she woke to hear Vic's half-suppressed gasps of pain. When he shook his head without speaking, she rang the emergency services and was told if she could get a friend to drive him to St Helier's, it would probably be quicker than waiting for an ambulance.

'I'm only sorry it had to be you, Michael,' she finished.

'Joan,' I said, 'I'm sorry it happened at all but since it did, I'm not a bit sorry you called me.' And she managed to give me a lopsided smile before she turned back and put a protective arm around Vic's shoulders. His eyes were closed and as we approached the Rose Hill roundabout, she told me it was his second heart attack in a year and the doctor she spoke to thought it was serious enough to make waiting for an ambulance risky. We watched him being wheeled into the intensive care unit and sat in the waiting room, somehow finding ourselves clutching half emptied plastic teacups. In response to her thanks, I said again I was glad to help and how much I owed to her and Vic but the half-remembered dream and the bang on the head had drained me and I was glad when the nurse returned to tell Joan that Vic was out of danger. She told us he would almost certainly sleep for the next few hours. The best thing Joan could do is to get some rest too and come back about eight o'clock with his clothes and shaving kit. I drove her back to the flats, patted the back of her hand, and again muttered something about how much I owed her and Vic. Then I asked if she'd be all right and told her I was going back to bed.

'Let me know how he is,' I said as I left her at her front door. 'I'll give you a ring from the factory later in the day.' She wasn't looking at me as I spoke and glancing back at her when I reached my flat, I saw she hadn't moved. Calling myself all sorts of a bloody idiot, I went back and took her hand.

'Come on, you soppy ha'porth,' I said. 'We'll have a cup of tea together.'

We sat side by side on the old couch and when she stopped shaking and began to cry, I held her until she fell asleep with her head against my cheek. The way Margery cried herself to sleep after her mother died. The way I cried into my pillow after Margery. When Joan woke up and looked startled until she realised where she was, she sat up and asked, 'Is it worth it, Michael? Is it worth letting yourself get so close to someone, they can break your heart by dying?'

'I think it is,' I said as much to myself as to her. 'Maybe once in a lifetime it can be worthwhile.' To stop myself thinking about Margery's death and what it was still doing to me, I put the kettle on for another cup of tea and rang the hospital.

'She said he's already sitting up and taking notice,' I told Joan. 'You'll see. The pair of you will be showing off your song and dance act at George's wedding yet.'

I dropped her off at St Helier's on my way to the factory where I was determined to sneak into my office for a quiet half hour before facing the world. Sod's law being in full working order, I got out of the car to find Henry, my friendly quality controller, waiting for me.

'It's about time you turned up,' he bellowed in my ear. 'I can't pass these coats. You gave me a docket of 500 to go out to the warehouse this morning. There's cottons hanging everywhere, the labels have been sewn on crooked, and there's not a single garment that's been properly pressed off! Don't you ever take the effing trouble to look at the effing work before you send it down to my passers?'

I managed to suppress a yawn and put my hand on his shoulder. 'What's happened to good morning, Henry?' I asked before letting a maddened Crazy Bear get at him. 'Can't you at least say good morning before you start a fight with me? I'm having a pretty shitty day up to now.'

'So what sort of a day do you think I'm having?' he bawled. 'To me every day is a shitty day. I got three passers cutting the cottons off your coats and steaming out the sodding gloss marks. It's not their job to clean coats and be pressers. You know bloody well it isn't.'

'Get away with you,' I said, walking with him into the passing section. 'They're lucky to have jobs, the way this lousy business is going.'

Mollified, he laughed and punched me lightly on the arm. 'Your daddy used to say that in the days it was true.' I returned the smile and nodded an acknowledgement at the passer who put a coat on a stand and for my benefit, elaborately cut off a stray cotton.

'Henry,' I asked, 'how would you and Lyn like to come to George's wedding next month?'

'We were there when you married your lovely Margery, weren't we? Why wouldn't we want to come to George's wedding? I just hope he's found himself as beautiful a bride as yours was.'

I promised to have a go at the pressers and the finishers in the factory about the coats, patted Henry on the shoulder, and kept the smile fixed to my face until I got into the office. He hadn't said what he said to hurt me. No one ever did say things to hurt me. If I had a problem every time I was reminded of how Margery looked when we were young marrieds and how changed she was by her illness, it was my hang up, mine and Crazy Bear's, not theirs. By now I should have the right attitude to death. Margery's death. My death. Vic's.

68

Anybody's. Like Joan had when she told me she talked to Margery's photograph and I mustn't change the frame because Margery wouldn't like it. Like Doctor Patel had when he came to the flat to check me over and stayed for a cup of tea. Right thinking leads to the right attitude and right deeds. There comes a time to stop feeling guilty and begin to feel and act positive.

'After all,' Patel said while I could feel him watching for my reaction, 'you weren't thinking about your late wife when you were enjoying the other lady. The problems came later.'

'Enjoying is a nice word for it,' I told him. 'I was brought up to use a different one. Don't you ever use a dirty word?'

'Did you think you were doing a dirty thing?' he asked and I stared back at him, not knowing how to answer.

I sat behind my desk, spent half an hour catching up with the mail and work dockets that were overflowing my in-tray, had a word with Bobby on the intercom, and invited myself to the cutting room for coffee. I told him about Vic when I walked in and accepted the cup he handed me. After I promised to let him and Delia know how the old boy was getting on, I said, 'Talking about old boys, Henry had another go at me when I got in. The coats were nothing like as bad as he made out but maybe they could do with a little more tender loving care before they come down to the passers.'

Bobby looked up from his patterns and frowned. 'For the price we get? Come on, Michael. You know damn well they'd have gone in to the warehouses as they were. The old bugger's asserting himself again. Perhaps it's time we had a chat about letting him go. He is getting on a bit, you know.'

I blew on my scalding coffee and looked at him. 'The truth is, Bobby, the old bugger's getting on a lot. It's just that I was hoping he'd make his own mind up about the right time to quit. I'd hate to see him off after all these years.'

'I wouldn't hate to see him off,' Bobby said savagely. 'I'd kick him out this minute. Do you know how long those two delivery vans in the yard have been waiting to load up? Do you know what it's costing us in driver hours when we can't get a docket of work past the old sod?'

I nodded to indicate that I knew and swallowed the last of the coffee. 'All right, I'll call him in the office and tell him now. We might as well get it over with.'

'Okay and thanks,' said Bobby. He grinned suddenly and laid a hand over mine. 'Take it easy with him. I'm fond of the old bastard too, you know.'

I took it as easy as I knew how. Henry took it as hard as he knew how. I told him not to get upset, it was bad for his health. I had seen one heart attack that morning and I didn't want to see another, thank you very much. Henry wasn't listening to a word I had to say. He was far too busy shouting about Bobby and me being a pair of ungrateful bastards who weren't fit to lick our father's boots and I knew where I could shove his retirement pension and he prayed to God it would be stuck up there forever. By the time he had thrown himself out of my office and slammed the door behind him, Crazy Bear was an incoherent maniac, my head was thumping a tattoo behind my eyes, and I was glad to get the hell out of there and meet Sara for lunch.

'Just eat and don't you dare ask me what sort of day I'm having. I might just tell you.'

'Thank you,' she said, smiling sweetly as she seated herself, 'and what sort of day have you been having?' After I told her about Joan and Vic and managed to stop her galloping off the hospital to see how he was for herself, I found myself talking about seventy-three-year old Henry Leaman.

'Henry began working for our father when they were both young men. He helped dad build the business up from nothing and when his wife Lyn wasn't working in the factory, she helped to bring up Bobby and me. The trouble is times change. It's not the same business any more. Henry can't or won't understand that our factory methods have to change with them.' Warming to the subject, I began to tell her about costings and margins and how it was impossible to work to a price when that silly old sod kept transport and drivers idling in the yard while he and his passers piddled about trying to make coats we were getting peanuts for into a load of bloody masterpieces.

'Bobby and I try to tell him the work has to go out when the drivers are ready to load. Dad used to say the same thing. It's no good promising the customer gold tomorrow. If you agreed to send a docket of coats in today, send it, even if it's only silver plated..'

I looked up to see Sara smiling and wanted to know what was so damn funny all of a sudden. I was having one hell of a day. I deserted Joan at her front door without seeing how badly she needed some company. I upset an old friend I'd known all my life. I was just about ready to go home and hide under the sheets before I screwed someone else's life up and she was grinning. What right did she have to grin at me, I demanded to know?

Sara laughed aloud. 'I'm sorry Michael,' she said, 'I can't help it. You're such an idiot when you feel sorry for yourself.'

I put down my knife and fork and glared at her. 'What makes you think I feel sorry for myself for Christ's sake? I'm feeling sorry for Joan and Vic and poor old Henry Leaman. There's nothing wrong with me. I'm all right, I'm doing fine. In every way on every day and all that load of crap.'

Sara leaned across the table to pat my hand. 'Are you, Michael? Are you really? All you've done since we sat down is blame yourself for other people's problems. You almost certainly saved Vic's life this morning. It's not your fault you didn't see at once how badly Joan was reacting to going home to pack him a suitcase. What matters is, you did see and you did the right thing. As for the old man in your factory not keeping up with the times, you should see me struggling with my new computer. I dare say the two of us should have been shown the door years ago.'

'Do you really think I feel sorry for myself?' I asked.

'There are times we all feel sorry for ourselves. I felt sorry for myself when I took Julie to try on her bridesmaid's dress. She says it's got too many frills and it makes her look like a little girl.'

'She is a little girl.'

'Why don't you come over and tell her that on Saturday? She'll love you for it.'

I took Sara's hand. 'Do you know what I'd like to come over there and do right now?'

'I can guess,' she said. 'Have some chocolate profiteroles instead. They'll fatten you up and take your mind off it.'

'You made me try that last week,' I told her. 'It didn't work then either. Chocolate makes me come over all unnecessary.'

I escorted her back to her office, kissed her on the cheek, wished her luck with her new computer, and drove on to the factory. The delivery vans had gone, the passers were wearing long faces and tutting over the latest docket to come down from the factory, and Henry Leaman sat in my office dividing his time between filling my ashtray with half smoked butts and chewing what was left of his finger nails.

'Listen Michael,' he said when I walked past him and hung up my jacket. 'I didn't mean what I said. Not about you and Bobby. Not about the pension either. Lyn and I knew the day had to come sometime and it's good of the two of you to want to give me so much. I should be thanking you, not insulting you.'

'You've called me worse than that, you miserable old sod,' I replied. 'The number of things you've told me to stick up my arse would keep me constipated the rest of my life. Besides, the thanks go the other way. Without you there wouldn't be a business. Bobby and I both know that.'

Henry shrugged. 'Maybe, maybe not. There were times I didn't get on so well with your daddy either. When do you want me to go? Tonight? The end of the week?'

'Only when it suits you. Why not leave it till after the wedding? You haven't changed your mind about coming to see George married, have you?'

Henry looked shocked. 'You think Lyn would let me? She cried her heart out for your Margery when she died. You think she doesn't want to see you have a little happiness for a change?'

After he said it, I couldn't wait for him to get out of the office and leave me to myself for a while. I hadn't known that George's wedding was supposed to give me a little happiness for a change. I looked at Henry's screwed up cigarette ends and became sorry I'd given up smoking. To stop myself from picking one of the larger ones up and lighting it, I emptied the ashtray, opened a window to clear the air, and poured myself a drink instead.

The following Saturday morning, I went to Sara's flat and saw Julie's dress. Designed by the bride's mother who, I sincerely hoped, had no hand in her daughter's gown, it hung on the back of the wardrobe looking like nothing so much as a very short and very wide Michelin man made of pink cake frills. The child hated it.

'Tell you what,' I said to her, 'I just happen to know a lady who can design and make you a dress you'll love. Let's all of us go up west and match the material. Then I'll take you to meet the fantabulous Lynda Leaman.'

Julie's eyes opened wide. 'Could we? Could we really get a different dress, Uncle Michael?'

'You go on calling me Uncle Michael, you get a pair of shoes to match.'

'But what about this monstrosity?' asked Sara. 'I wouldn't want to upset your George's new in-laws over it.'

'Accidents can happen in the best regulated circles,' I said, smiling at Julie and for the first time since I met the child, getting a smile in return. And she kept on smiling when Lyn Leaman folded her arms and said severely that she'd put her thimble away years ago but for a little sweetheart like Julie, she supposed she'd have to get the darned thing out again.'

Chapter Twelve

I collected our wedding gear from Moss Bros and Dicky came down from Manchester to spend the night before the wedding on my couch. It was a kind of making up between us and, although neither he nor I mentioned the night I came home drunk and punched him in the face, I was glad to have his company. While he was there, I telephoned Clara, George's future mother-in-law, and told her about the accident I had with Julie's dress, catching the hem in the car door and ripping it. I told her how upset the child was, how devastated I was, but thank goodness a friend came to the rescue and loaned Julie a beautiful pink bridesmaid's dress that was almost as nice as the original.

'No,' I agreed, soberly watching a doubled up Crazy Bear slapping his thighs and howling with laughter, 'of course it couldn't be anything like as pretty as the one you designed for her. I was just saying that in the hope it might make you feel a touch better about the accident. Honestly Clara, I can't tell you how sorry I am for being so clumsy. Julie's mother is absolutely furious with me. Oh yes, it's exactly the same shade of pink. I can at least promise you that.'

There was more of the same. Much more. I too hoped that the makeshift dress wouldn't spoil her only daughter's great day. I fervently agreed that it would almost certainly ruin the photographs. Wishing I could send Crazy Bear down the wire to split her in two, I begged the gently weeping Clara not to be too upset.

'She's still a pretty little girl,' I said. 'She still looks very nice.'

'But she would have looked beautiful,' wept Clara. 'It's such a shame. My Ted wants to speak to you.'

'Yes,' I agreed with good old Ted. 'It is a shame to upset Clara with bad news the night before Donna's wedding.' Of course I understood that an only daughter's wedding is a very emotional time for her mother and father. When he allowed me to speak, I told him I was trying to save them the shock of seeing Julie arrive in the wrong dress. That was the reason I rang.

'Of course I'm sorry,' I finished abjectly, 'and of course I can appreciate that Clara will want to look her best tomorrow. I'm quite sure she will. If I may say so, she is a very attractive lady. You are a lucky man. Why yes Ted, of course you can tell Clara I think you're a lucky man. I envy you. I really do.'

At last it was over. I put the phone down, grinned shamefacedly at Dicky, and told him the story of Julie's dress and the lengths I'd gone to in matching the material and getting Lyn Leaman to make her a new one.

When he'd done laughing he said, 'and I suppose you'd rather be in Julie's good books than worry about George's new in-laws.' I glared for a moment and then, confessing that I supposed I would, laughed with him. Julie's opinion mattered to me.

'I like Mrs Leighton,' Dicky said, changing the subject. 'I think she'd be good for you. You spend too much time alone.'

'Brooding with a bottle, you mean.'

'I didn't say that, dad. I know it's hard for you to talk about things but George and I aren't stupid. You've changed a lot since mum died. We know how lonely you've been these last few years. For some time we've been thinking you could do with a friend. Preferably a lady friend. If you promise not to get angry, I'll tell you something else.'

'Give me a drink first,' I said. 'I never try to hit people if there's a chance I might spill a drink.'

He smiled, poured a small whisky, and drowned it with soda before handing it to me. 'We sent your details to a marriage bureau, care of George's address. It cost us over a hundred quid. I was going to tell you about it the morning I came up and found Mrs Leighton in the kitchen.'

'Richard Brent,' I said after draining the drink, 'you and your brother George are a pair of right raving nutters.'

'Yes daddy,' he replied meekly. 'We know.'

I shook my head at him, said good night, and went into the bedroom. Dicky had elected to keep me company rather than attend George's stag night and George had sworn to join us around nine o'clock the next morning. Our three examples of Moss Bros best grey morning suits were hanging on the wardrobe. Ted had arranged for a car to collect us, including Joan and Vic, who was now out of hospital and refusing to be left out of the proceedings, at a precise eleven fourteen.

'Eleven fourteen, Ted?' I repeated when he told me over a pint at his local.

'I'm glad you picked up on that, Michael, my old son,' he said, beaming at me. 'It's the way I keep these people on their toes. Eleven fifteen is the same as eleven thirty to them. Tell them a minute earlier, the buggers think they're on such a tight schedule they turn up on the dot. It works every time. You wait and see.'

'Well I'm blessed, Ted, my old son,' I said as we enthusiastically clinked glasses. 'What a brilliant idea. Of course I'll wait and see.'

Maybe it was Dicky's company or the fact I hadn't had a drink to speak of that I had the best night's sleep I'd had in years. I came out of the bedroom clear eyed and bushy tailed. Just in time to see Dicky letting in a hollow eyed George who showered, borrowed my razor, and in between mouthfuls of toast and gulps at a steaming mug of coffee, swore he couldn't eat a thing. He and Dicky, two soggy blobs of pre-wedding nerves, laughed hysterically when I told them they had to be ready for the car at eleven fourteen precisely or good old Ted was calling off the wedding. By the time the car put in an appearance at a quarter to twelve, Crazy Bear was on his back kicking his legs in the air and the boys were sobbing with laughter. Vic, who had lost more than a stone in weight during his stint in hospital and still looked pale and ill, was forced to walk slowly and cling to Joan's arm. We arrived at the church fifteen minutes late.

Leaving Joan and Vic to follow at their own pace, George, Dicky, and I leapt from the car and scurried into the church to a shrill, 'Darlings, for heaven's sake! What kept you?' from Delia, who insisted on inspecting the three of us and further flustering George by adjusting his tie and half throttling him. As we walked down the aisle, Henry Leaman bobbed up to pump the bridegroom's hand up and down and wish him all the luck in the world, while his seventy-two-year-old wife, Lyn, stretched up for a kiss and said, 'You've still got time to make your own luck, darling. This could be your last chance to kiss an experienced woman.'

'With a last chance like you,' Henry growled while George put his arms round Lyn and kissed her cheek, 'he should be so lucky.'

As soon as George, Dicky and I settled in the front pew, I glanced over my shoulder for Sara. To my surprise, she was nowhere to be seen. I raised my eyebrows and asked Delia who said she hadn't seen her either but she was probably with Julie and the bride.

Bobby and Delia sat immediately behind us, her making a fashion statement and looking stunning in a fitted navy blue costume and matching straw hat with a wide white ribbon hatband. Margery's parents, who spent the night with Delia and Bobby and were sitting beside them, leaned across the back of the pew to shake hands and give George a small white envelope. Containing an appropriate cheque, of course. Fat chance of my straight-laced father-in-law handing over an envelope with a French letter or a smutty rhyme about Eskimo Nell tucked inside it. George kissed his grandmother, shook his grandfather's hand, and handed the envelope to Dicky for safe keeping.

As more and more guests arrived and the hubbub in the church grew louder, Clara bustled down the aisle wearing a blue and pink flowered dress and a mushroom shaped hat of the same material, an outfit that served to make her look plumper than ever. She came over to give Delia's clothes a sharp look before standing on tiptoe to kiss George and me and to tell me she had inspected Julie's dress. It was much too plain, of course, and it did nothing at all for the poor child, but at least the colour wasn't too dreadful and her little bouquet wouldn't look too out of place. She hadn't forgiven me yet, she said with a coquettish sideways glance, but she could see I'd done my best to repair the damage.

I gave her arm an affectionate little squeeze and murmured, 'I'm truly sorry it happened but you mustn't let an accident spoil the day for you, Clara. It's the mother of the bride they'll be looking at. Ted told me on the telephone you look beautiful today. I can see he's a man who knows what he's talking about.'

'Silly old Michael,' she said, coyly returning the squeeze. 'You know perfectly well they won't be looking at me, they'll all be watching the bride. But I'm glad you like me. I really do want you to like me.' She gazed up at me for a soulful moment before scuttling off to speak to people on the other side of the aisle.

'She's a bit of all right,' Bobby said, poking me in the back as I sat down. 'Anyone can see she fancies you. How you're the one who gets the girls every time beats the hell out of me.'

'Don't start getting jealous,' I said over my shoulder. 'You want her, you can have her gift wrapped.'

'She's already gift wrapped,' he muttered. 'How would I get her out of it all before I fell asleep?' Sending Dicky into a fit of giggles he fought to control until it was cut short by the vicar calling him and George to stand before him. The organist began the wedding march and the crowd shuffled and turned to watch a beaming Ted match his steps to Donna's as he escorted her down the aisle, followed by a white faced, terrified Julie whose tightly clenched fingers threatened to choke the life out of the small posy she held out straight before her.

I looked at George and Dicky, tall and elegant in their grey morning suits. Donna the bride, tiny and very pretty beside her beetroot faced father's bulk. A little way behind stood Julie, the colour returning to her cheeks as she began to enjoy the attention she was getting. The vicar smiled broadly at the bride and groom and took two or three deep breaths as he prepared to take the service. And when Crazy Bear appeared and squatted at my feet, there came the moment I needed Margery more than ever. She was my wife for God's sake. She was supposed to be sitting beside me, snuffling into my handkerchief to show how happy she was. I tried to see and feel her filling the emptiness at my side. Dressed in something red. She loved wearing red. She'd be digging her scarlet tipped fingernails into the back of my hand to make me sit up straight and pay due attention to our son's wedding. Which was happening right now and please God never to happen again. At least, not because one of them dies before their time. Margery Brent, the beautiful mother of the bridegroom, wanted me, his done up to the nines father, to concentrate on every aspect of the ceremony. So we could talk about it when we got home. Sharing the memories while we cuddled and made love and lived happily ever after, amen.

Or maybe she was digging her nails into my wrist to slow me down. To make me relax and to stop the buzzing in my head. To stop me remembering that one day Dicky would get married and she wouldn't be sitting beside me there, either. There would be grandchildren she'd never know. A future she would never be a part of. Margery robbed of half her life and knowing nothing of the half of mine I was being forced to live without her.

Suddenly, Crazy Bear shifted uneasily and looked up through the stained glass window for the sky. I began to panic with him, feeling his need to get out of the church and into the sunshine. Without thinking, I turned to rise and found myself looking at Julie. The child wore a chaplet of white and pink flowers on her head. The dress Lyn made for her had a neat bodice, cut high beneath her incipient bust, and the skirt was full and flounced at the hem. To steady my nerves, I saw myself cutting the pattern. Laying out the heavy pattern paper on the old cutting bench dad taught Bobby and me on. I visualized marking out the neck to waist, the waist to hem, the flare of the skirt, the shape of the puffed sleeves. Knowing by what our dad would call rock of eye, exactly how much fullness to let into the armhole.

Sensing that I was looking at her, Julie turned her head and smiled at me. I managed the best smile I could return to her and then slumped back on the bench to stare at my sons' backs while Dicky handed the wedding ring to George and George and Donna made their vows. And while I watched, I dug the fingernails of my right hand into my left wrist and thought about Margery doing the same to stop herself getting over-emotional when we watched something sad on television or in the theatre.

Watched something sad? How about this bloody charade? The truth was Margery never knew the meaning of sad. No one knew the meaning of sad. Not this kind of sad. Someone spoke and touched my elbow. Obediently I stood up and accompanied Ted and Clara and George and Donna to sign the marriage certificate. I kissed Donna's cheek and shook George's hand. Clara gripped my arms and kissed me on the mouth. Good old Ted shook my hand and slapped my back.

'Cheer up my son,' said good old Ted, 'it might never happen.'

I thought better of telling him it already had. The moron wouldn't have understood me and anyway, it was George and Donna's wedding day. I grinned feebly and suffered another slap on the back without allowing Crazy Bear to split him in two. For a moment I thought of slapping him in retaliation but the war could wait until the party was over. I followed him and the rest of the wedding group I had to remind myself I was part of, out of the vestry and into the main body of the church. Crazy Bear stiffened and drew his hunting knife when we saw Paul Leighton step out of the shadow of a pillar.

The difference in his appearance from the last time I saw him was remarkable. Now, his hair was well brushed and he carried what looked like a new hat in his left hand. He wore a navy blue suit and an impeccably ironed white shirt. His blue and red striped tie had been expertly knotted and his shoes were highly polished. Of Sara, there was no sign at all.

'Come on, groom's dad. You have to be in the picture too,' the photographer was shouting at me as I stopped to face Paul. 'We need all the family for the first group.'

Paul neatly sidestepped Crazy Bear and came close. 'Congratulations,' he said, holding out a hand and showing a gleam of teeth. 'You've got two fine sons and a beautiful daughter-in-law.'

'So what do I want your wife and daughter for..' I had almost finished for him when he went on to say, 'Look, Michael, I'm sorry to bother you with this but Sara and I need your help. I've persuaded her to try for a reconciliation. We're having a few days in Cornwall and she's gone home to pack. Do you think your sister-in-law would look after Julie until we come back? Here are the keys to the flat. We'll leave Julie's bag in the hall.'

The congregation crowded me towards the open doors and the photographer was yelling. All I could take in was the fact that Sarah had deserted me. Brushing Paul's fingers with my own, I took the keys and walked out into the sunshine to smile for the birdy..

Chapter Thirteen

The wedding reception was held in Ted and Clara's large back garden. They had hired a marquee, inside which were gold backed chairs, circular plastic tables for the hundred or so guests, and a top table for the immediate families. Ted, Clara, Dicky and I sat each side of the bride and groom, presumably to stop George making a run for it before it was too late. There were table decorations, floating pink and gold ribbons, balloons, and a keyboard player cum singer who was a cousin of Clara's and kept apologizing for not being in good voice today, folks, I guess I'm a little nervous, but don't let that spoil your enjoyment of the occasion. To eat, there was a curl of ham on a lettuce leaf starter, followed by a main course of chicken salad, followed by a wedge of something cold and tart with ice cream, followed by coffee, chocolate mints, and a slice off the three tier wedding cake. In front of me stood a bottle of whisky. Delia whipped it away before I could lay a finger on the damned thing. I was decorously sipping an insipid semi sweet white wine, listening to the chatter of the crowd, and glaring poison darts at my sister-in-law who was smiling sweetly back at me when Ted stopped the keyboard player's barely recognizable rendition of 'Hello Dolly' and stood up to make a speech welcoming the guests. While he tearfully thanked everyone there for helping him and his wonderful wife Clara celebrate their darling daughter's wedding and it only seemed like yesterday when he collected his little darling and her wonderful mother from the maternity hospital, I remembered he'd asked me to propose the health of the bride and groom. Ted finished his piece with a dirty joke about the way Martians need three participants and a very wide bed to make love in and, while Clara made goo goo eyes in my direction, welcomed me and George into the bosom of his family. Someone, thinking it was another joke, laughed at that, too.

'Well,' I said, standing up with my glass in my hand, 'how do I follow that?'

'How about the story you tell about the Venutions and their convolutions?' yelled Henry Leaman, who'd either been a lot luckier with the booze than I had or had forgotten it was the same story.

'Don't make trouble,' I warned him, 'or I'll have to sort you out in the factory on Monday morning.'

Henry laughed. 'No you won't, mate. I retired yesterday and all you've got go do is pay me my pension.'

'All right,' I said amid the general laughter, 'you're retired. Just don't forget I know where you live. If I think you're getting lazy, I can always send along a couple of rails of coats.'

I went on to say all the right things. How beautiful Donna was and what a lovely bride and not too bad looking groom she and George made in church. How pretty Julie was, how proud I was of my sons, how thrilled my late wife Margery would have been, and what a wonderful wedding breakfast Ted and his lovely wife Clara had given us all. In the best toastmaster tradition, I asked them all to be upstanding and drink the health of the bride and groom. Which they did while the trusty keyboard player led them in two choruses of for they are jolly good fellows, followed by three cheers, repeated because he said he couldn't hear them the first time. I sent Crazy Bear across to wrap his tinny sounding plastic keyboard round his neck so I could sit down. Which I eventually did and got a kiss on the cheek from Donna and a pat on the back of the hand from George, who whispered, 'Well done, Dad.' I grinned back at both of them. I thought I'd done pretty well too. Sara not being there to curb me, I thought I'd done enough to justify a small whisky.

What remained of the reception passed in a rosy enough glow. Me passing on Paul Leighton's request to Delia who said yes, of course she'd look after Julie if Sara wanted her to but looked as if she didn't believe a word of it. Me telling myself the look wasn't because I'd been dumped in favour of Paul. It was because she would have expected Sara to ask her herself. Good old Ted, giving me and the bottle I was clutching a look that said he hoped George wasn't going to turn out like me. Me again, stumbling over Donna when she tried to dance with me. Donna, looking anxiously up into my face while she tried to keep the full skirt of her wedding dress clear of my clumsy feet. Me again, singing along with the miraculously improved keyboard player while Donna and George disappeared into Ted and Clara's house. Re-emerging half an hour later in their going away clothes. Driving off to their honeymoon and the start of a new life where they would be happy ever after because the sun never sets and nobody ever dies and people didn't have to muddle through alone and why the fuck had Sara gone off with her ex-husband after she told me how much she hated the bastard?

I sprawled on one of the golden chairs, fretted at the problem for a while, and poured myself another drink. George was fixed up for the night. He and Donna were on their honeymoon. Bobby was more than all right with Delia. Vic could have it off with Joan if she wasn't too worried about his damaged heart. Ted would all right, if he stayed awake long enough to get his Clara out of her corset. Even Henry Leaman was all right if they still did it at his age. Every one of them with a bed warmer to shag. So why did it all go wrong for me? Maybe it was seeing Julie all dressed up and looking pretty in the dress Lyn made that brought Sara and Paul round to the idea of reconciliation. I shook my head sadly and gave myself another whisky. I'd been stupid. If I'd let Julie wear the Michelin man dress, maybe I'd have had someone to take home and shag. Someone to save me from being alone with my collection of nightmares for a night.

Vic and Joan drove Dicky and me and George's clothes from Moss Bros home and Vic said no, I hadn't been too bad, not really. Maybe a bit too loud when the keyboard player rounded off the party by mangling the Anniversary Waltz. Not that anybody could dance in a crowded marquee anyway. It was no wonder a table or two got knocked over. Things were better when they rolled up the sides and let a little air in. Joan wasn't speaking. She sat very straight with her lips pressed together and not looking at me. Suddenly feeling stone cold and very sober, I asked who caught the bride's bouquet.

'You did, you berk,' said Vic, and you refused to give it up.'

'Ah,' I said, beginning to remember. 'I didn't happen to sing something about me marrying Prince Charming and Prince Charming marrying me, did I?' The stiffness of Joan's back and Dicky's shamefaced grin told me I had sung the song. The army version.

Margery's parents came to pick Dicky up the next morning. They were dropping him off in Manchester on their way home to Leeds. I gave them a coffee while he packed his rucksack. I sat with them and agreed with Margery's mum that the wedding had been lovely, that Donna was beautiful and George looked handsome, that Ted and Clara were a lovely couple, the food was lovely, and so was the wedding cake. My mother-in-law looked like Margery in a greying, faded kind of way. Given a full life, I supposed Margery would have grown to look like her, but there the comparison ended. My wife didn't say people were lovely very often and she certainly wouldn't have said it about good old Ted and Clara. She might well have said it about her parents' home in Leeds. Margery could be deep. The last time we were at the Festival Hall we looked at an exhibition of paintings. She walked past most of the blob and splotch efforts and then stopped. Putting on her reading glasses, she stood with her head on one side studying a view of a garden seen through the blown apart net curtains of a bedroom window. The foreground showed a neat lawn edged by a path, a rockery, and a pair of wooden benches. At the back, the sun shone through the branches of a blossoming apple tree that looked as if it straddled the back fence. Beyond the garden were the red roofs and chimneys of houses in the next street. Margery smiled at me and said it reminded her of looking through her bedroom window when she was an innocent young maiden.

'You mean before you knew me?' I asked. 'Was I that much of a shock?'

The smile deepened. 'Just a bit.'

I was drinking my coffee, thinking of the painting, half listening to Margery's mum, and remembering that I'd promised to take Margery back to Leeds one day and now I never would when my father-in-law cleared his throat and said he was watching me in church. He thought I looked lonely. He and her mother missed Margery, we all did, it was only natural. But I had to learn to let go eventually and begin picking up the pieces, however hard it was to do. I looked at him, Margery's dad who never really took to me or thought I was halfway good enough for his daughter. He was the last person I thought would understand but he did and I shook his hand with real warmth when they left, closing the door on me and three rather crumpled Moss Brother's grey morning suits, shirts, cravats, and top hats.

I drank a toast to the lot of them, picked up the telephone and rang Sara's number just in case she'd changed her mind about going off with Paul. There was no reply so the Moss brothers and I drank to another happy couple.

Chapter Fourteen

I returned our wedding glad rags to the Brothers Moss and was on my way home for a belated breakfast when I made myself remember that the Leightons had gone to Cornwall to kiss and make up. Thanks to them, I'd had a lousy night, I wanted to forget that Sara ever happened, but I had promised to collect Julie's suitcase and Delia would be expecting me to deliver it. Resenting the necessity, I drove to the flat and let myself in. Without Sara to greet me, it was dark and alien and full of wrong memories. All I wanted was to snatch up the child's suitcase and get out of there but it wasn't in the hall as Paul had promised. I swore aloud and looked for it in the kitchen and the dining room before entering the bedroom and walking into another of my worst nightmares.

From nowhere, a school satchel hit me across the back of my head. I reeled and fell to my knees, seeing the stars I saw and hearing the laughter I heard when I lay grovelling in the school playground begging the big boys not to hit me again. Hearing Crazy Bear's scream of outrage at the realization that we'd been ambushed, I scrabbled round to face my attacker, throwing up my hand as the satchel came down again, knocking me to the floor as a shoe connected with the point of my chin. I was getting to my knees, shaking the dizziness out of my head and trying to wipe tears from my eyes, when I heard the front door close and knew whoever had attacked me was gone.

The bedroom curtains were drawn but I could see someone on the bed and knew it had to be Sara. Unusually for a fidget like her, she lay on her back, quite still, with the covers drawn to her chin and her eyes closed. Crazy Bear came to squat beside me and together we stared at her. For the moment we thought she was asleep and were glad she'd missed the fracas. Glad too that the attempted reconciliation couldn't have worked out and she must have sent Paul away. When, by mutual consent, Crazy Bear put out a hand to smooth her hair back from her forehead and I lifted the covers away from her face, we saw that she was dead. And as I felt the blood drain from my face and the world became black and empty, I fainted.

With no idea of how long I remained unconscious, I came to and forced myself to open my eyes. Somehow, I'd wedged myself between the bed and the wall. My knees were drawn up to my chin and I was gripping Sara's bedding between both clenched fists. Compulsively throwing it from me, I struggled to my feet, turned my head away from the body, and stumbled out of the bedroom and into the kitchen. The crazy buzz I'd been living with since Margery died had amplified into something louder and more uneven in my ears. I retched, knowing I'd vomited somewhere, probably on the bedroom floor, and was forced to rinse the taste out of my mouth before I could stop shaking and dry my eyes. By the time I dialled three nines and told the police what I'd found, the buzz had reached the pit of my stomach and begun churning.

I heard them coming from a long way off. When the siren stopped and two capped and uniformed policemen walked into the flat, I indicated the bedroom and told them no, I didn't think I could go back in there with them. Then I leaned against the kitchen wall and tried not to imagine what they were doing and what they were looking at while floorboards creaked, a chair scraped against the door, and the officers spoke quietly to each other. The one who came back to the dining room to ask me questions I couldn't hear properly had taken off his cap. I looked at the top of his bald head and answered with a shrug or a nod and was left alone until the party was joined by a dark skinned man wearing a business suit.

'The body's in there, sergeant,' said the policeman who had spoken to me. Together we watched him enter Sara's bedroom and when after a few minutes, he returned, he said to me, 'I am Detective Sergeant Ginney. So far, all I know about the death is that you are Mr Michael Brent, you discovered the body, and you dialled 999 and reported your discovery to the police.'

I nodded my head.

'Did you live in this flat with the deceased, Mr Brent?'

I shook my head.

'I see.' He made a note and went on to ask if I had touched anything in the bedroom and was there any more I was able to tell him about the incident. I could hear the tremor in my voice when I told him I didn't think there was anything I could tell him about what happened in the bedroom. Yes, of course I knew the deceased. We were friends. Yes, very good friends. I thought she had gone away for a short holiday. How long had I been in the flat before making the call? I didn't know, not really. I had the key and came in to collect Julie's suitcase, which was supposed to be in the hall. I couldn't find it so I went into the bedroom and found Sara. When I saw she was dead, I must have passed out. Oh yes, I did touch something. I pulled back her blankets and I thought I was sick on the floor. When I came in, I thought she was asleep. I thought she'd changed her mind about leaving me and going back to her ex-husband. I must have touched her. I was trying to wake her up. I wanted to know what the hell was going on but when I saw…when I saw…when I saw…when…

'Now you just steady on sir,' said the sergeant, who'd made no attempt to interrupt me while I was ranting. 'Perhaps you'd best sit over here and take a few deep breaths before we go any further. I'll get the constable to bring you a glass of water and when you're ready you can fill me in with a few details.'

'Details?' I repeated.

'What your precise relationship with the deceased was, when you last saw her alive, why you thought she was leaving you, who this Julie is, and the name of the ex-husband will do for a start. My inspector's on his way with the doctor and we can take a formal statement later.'

'Her husband is Paul Leighton,' I said clearly and distinctly. 'He's the man you want.' I sat down and immediately stood up again. 'He gave me the key to the front door and told me the suitcase would be in the hall. He meant me to search for it and find Sara dead. He killed her.'

The sergeant smiled gently. 'It's a bit early to talk about killing, isn't it sir? We don't yet know how the lady died. What makes you think her ex-husband would want to do her harm?'

To give them credit, once the police knew Sara had been strangled and Paul hadn't gone to Cornwall, they found him soon enough. Meanwhile Bobby came over from the factory to drive me home. A couple of hours after I waved him away and knocked the telephone off the hook, Sergeant Ginney was back with one of the constables to find me with a drink in my hand.

'Well now, Mr Brent,' he began. 'Mr Leighton has identified Mrs Leighton as his ex-wife Sara and during an informal interview at his home, made certain allegations against you.'

'Well he would,' I broke in. 'The whole exercise was meant to implicate me.'

'Mr Brent,' Ginney said patiently, 'if you are suggesting that Paul Leighton murdered his wife to get at you, no one is going to believe you. Not at this stage of the investigation, anyway. Why not hear me out and make your comments when I've finished?'

I nodded and learned that Paul, after recovering from the shock of seeing Sara on a mortuary slab, told the policeman who escorted him and then Sergeant Ginney that knowing the company she'd been keeping, he wasn't surprised it had come to this. He told them about the wedding Sara and Julie were going to. He knew about it because Julie kept him up to date on all her mother's affairs, especially the ones spelt with a capital A.

'I was the only affair...' I broke in – and stopped when Ginney held up a hand. He glanced at his notes and continued, 'Mr Leighton's daughter also told us about the upset you caused over the bridesmaid's dress she was supposed to wear at your son's wedding. Apparently, you deliberately ruined it.'

'That's a load of bullshit...' I began again and stopped, raising my hands when I saw Ginney's eyes on me. 'After questioning,' he went on, 'Mr Leighton said he wasn't sure why you spoiled the child's dress but at a guess, it was probably because you didn't want the child to be a bridesmaid. It would have given your sordid little game away. Unfortunately for you, your sister-in-law kicked up such a fuss when she heard about the spoiled dress, you were forced to spend a small fortune on having another one made for the child.'

I dropped my head in my hands and listened to the rest of it. Paul saying the silly episode with the dress would have given everyone a laugh if it wasn't for the lies I told. Julie told her father I said it was spoiled accidentally and the bride's parents were dreadfully upset. Tangled webs weren't in it. But then, the police probably knew about my drink problem. They didn't? Oh, but that was almost certainly the reason for my instability. No, Paul said in answer to further questioning, whatever I told the police about the key he was supposed to have given me, Sara had moved to the flat after the divorce. It was hardly likely he'd have a key to his estranged wife's front door.

Again no, he had not asked me or my sister-in-law to look after Julie. As a matter of fact, we were the very last people he would have dreamed of asking. He knew how hard we tried to poison Julie's mind against him. He knew all about the vicious lies I told. I denied it when, despite his attempts at reconciliation, his marriage had broken down and he discovered it was my fault. I was the one who set his wife against him and I tried to make Julie hate her father. Not that I could have got away with it. Young as she was, his Julie could see through Mr Michael Brent and his lies.

In answer to continued questioning, Paul had said he'd seen none of us for some time, he wasn't sure how long. Until the police called on him, he assumed that Julie was at home with her mother. No, of course he hadn't gone to the church to see the wedding. Much as he would have liked to have seen his daughter as a bridesmaid, he wasn't one to stick his oar in where it wasn't wanted. He repeated that Sara had never given him a key to the flat and he had never been inside the place.

If it helped the police at all, he could tell them I was violent. I'd threatened to beat him up on the one occasion we had met. He could see by the way I behaved I was mentally disturbed and he knew my wife had died quite young, he didn't know how, poor soul. No, he was not suggesting foul play, how could he when he didn't know what happened to her. He just thought it worth mentioning. Yes, of course it was one of the factors that worried him about my relationship with Sara.

That aside, now that he knew his poor dear wife was dead and Julie was with my sister-in-law, he would be taking his child out of harm's way the moment the police had finished asking him questions. No, he didn't mind cooperating with the officer. He just hoped I would be arrested and locked away before I did the same dreadful thing to some other innocent woman. His poor sweet Sara was always too trusting for her own good. Yes, it was true they were divorced but that had never been his wish and he would always think of her as his poor sweet Sara. His beloved wife. She was so beautiful. Then he burst into tears, read through his statement, and signed it.

Ginney closed his notebook and returned it to his pocket. 'Now listen to me, Mr Brent. While I do not necessarily accept what Mr Leighton has said, he's made an allegation and other statements about you that have to be shown to my Inspector along with the autopsy report. He will decide on what further action is to be taken.'

He and the constable got to their feet. 'I can trust you to be around when we want to speak to you again?' I nodded and they saw themselves out.

Two whiskies later, I saw a note fall on the mat, picked it up and read that my phone was off the hook. I dropped it back and picked it up to a call from Delia. 'That swine came for Julie,' she told me. 'Michael, he's evil, I know he is. I wanted to refuse but he said if I gave him any trouble, he'd tell the police I was trying to protect you because I knew you were Sara's killer and that would confirm everything he told them about you. The police have been here too. They asked if Bobby or I saw Paul either in the church or in its surrounds on the day of the wedding. The sergeant said I should consider my answer carefully because if it was yes, he would want to know where he was sitting and what he was wearing. I had to say no, darling. Neither of us saw him and Julie said she hadn't seen her daddy either.'

Nor had Vic and Joan seen me stop and speak to Paul. Vic came into my flat and told me a policeman had called in to ask them about the day. They told him that so far as they knew, they hadn't seen Paul Leighton. They weren't sure because they didn't really know what he looked like. No, they hadn't seen me stop to speak to anyone but the church was full and they, like the rest of the company, were looking at the bride, not me. All they saw me do after the ceremony was go outside for the family photographs.

After Vic shook his head to the offer of a drink and left, Crazy Bear folded his arms and stared at the wallpaper. I asked him what the fuck I was supposed to do now and without waiting for an answer, poured myself a drink and took it into the bedroom. I put my head on the pillow and faced Margery's photograph but as I dozed, I didn't dream about her. Not at first. Instead, I saw the dead Sara beneath her coverlet with the sheet drawn up to her chin, hiding her bruised throat and crooked arms. I stared at her curiously. Something about the way she lay reminded me of something or someone I'd seen before.

The sudden memory hit me with a shock that woke me and had me out of the bed and into the sitting room, curled on the couch, afraid to sleep. After Margery died, the boys took me away and sat me in a corridor. I got to my feet and followed other visitors to the hospice out to the street and into a store. Where I bought a pair of black shoes because rather than think of my wife's body twisted restlessly among the crumpled sheets, I had fixed my mind on her funeral.

George and Dicky found me standing on the roundabout with a shoe box under my arm and led me back into the hospice and into the side room by the multi faith chapel. Dicky was crying but when, instead of looking at Margery immediately, I tried to make sense of why I needed black shoes, George understood and patted my arm. I nodded and looked at the straightened body of my late wife. At peace, her eyes closed and her lips slightly parted showing a gleam of teeth, she had a spotless white sheet drawn up to her chin. And in my dream, she lay side by side with Sara's murdered body, lying in a distorted parody of the same position. For me they had become interchangeable. So unlike themselves in death as to be almost unrecognizable.

Like the bloodied anonymous bodies in a traffic accident I once saw. Lying beside a crushed car, the trapped driver of which screaming at the police driver who was trying to free her that she held him responsible for two deaths. The screams telling him he'd left her with nothing to live for. Telling him she might as well swallow some pills and kill herself.

I too was directly responsible for two deaths. I too might have left the dead Margery and the dead Sara by a crushed car. I too had nothing left to live for. And like all sick jokes, all I had in the medicine chest to commit suicide with was an out of date pack of indigestion tablets.

'It's the drink,' I told myself while I stood in the shower at three o'clock in the morning and scrubbed at the dirt. I thought I'd forgotten the motorway accident and the bodies with coats thrown over them. I never had an accident with a car. Not a real one. Just a coming out of a side road without looking where I was going on a wet Saturday afternoon prang that resulted in some slivers of orange glass and an angry, red faced man standing in front of me with clenched fists. A short plump man who was no more inclined to listen to my apology than he was to start a punch-up with an unknown quantity in the middle of the road. We stood there, two marshmallows facing each other down like turkey cocks until his wife broke the impasse by getting out of their car and demanding to see my insurance certificate and driver's licence, neither of which I had with me.

'Probably hasn't got one, I know the type,' my adversary said savagely before he extracted my promise to phone him with the details, which I did.

Whatever the dream meant, I have never had an accident in a car. Not one with Margery in it and not one with Sara in it. And I wasn't crippled like the woman who was trapped.

'But I'm crippled now,' I told myself while I stood under a cascade of steamy water and rubbed myself raw. 'Right here and now I'm crippled. I'm missing Margery and I'm missing Sara too and not just for her hot little twat.' Which was serious because before she was murdered, I'd almost convinced myself that her hot little twat was all she did mean to me. I turned off the shower and wiped the steam off the mirror to look at my reflection. Not caring for the look of the tragedy queen I faced, I said, 'Stop whining. You're going to marry Prince Charming, aren't you?. What more do you want?'

'Does Prince Charming have a twat?' asked Crazy Bear, whirling a tomahawk around my head.

'Sod off,' I said politely. I hadn't dried myself properly but I lay down on top of the bed and fell asleep wondering if I really had seen Paul Leighton in the church when everyone else said I hadn't because he wasn't there.

Chapter Fifteen

The ringing telephone woke me. It was Delia telling me through my yawns that they were coming over. No, she wouldn't take no for an answer. She and Bobby wanted to speak to me face to face and have me tell them exactly what happened in Sara's flat. The police wouldn't tell them a thing. All she knew was that Paul couldn't be trusted and who knew what was happening to Julie. He might be doing anything to the child. She said a lot more I didn't want to hear until she got to telling me they were on their way, whatever Bobby said.

'Which is?' I asked.

'That we should leave it alone and let the police sort it out. What do you think we should do?' I said leave it alone and let the police sort it out. She tutted and told me I was in one of my moods. Not that she was surprised by my moods, she knew me by now. I didn't need enemies to make trouble for me, I could make all the trouble I needed for myself. She'd have a word with Joan before they came. I wanted watching, I did. I was a bloody fool. She slammed the phone down before I had a chance to say I was joking, for Christ's sake. I was only making a lousy joke. The only reason I said it was because I hadn't had any breakfast yet. The police could do what they like with me, couldn't they? Maybe Scotland Yard kept tabs on me. Maybe they knew I'd not been punished for the way I treated my wife. They might think it only proper to punish me for killing Paul's wife instead.

It was a warm morning, the flat was stifling, and it was cooler to walk into the kitchen and make breakfast without troubling to get dressed. When Joan half opened the front door and asked if I was decent, I broke a couple of eggs in the frying pan and said, 'No, but come in anyway.'

'I thought you were joking,' she said, turning away after a glance. 'What's this for?'

I shrugged and went into the bedroom for a robe. 'Too hot to get dressed, that's all, Joannie. I wasn't after your body or anything like that.'

'I didn't think you were,' she said. 'It wouldn't be worth the trouble. Can I pour myself a cup of tea?'

I laughed and pushed the teapot across the table before asking if I'd been that much of a shock.

'No,' she said, sitting at the kitchen table to pour us both a cup, 'you weren't that much of a shock. I've got a good memory for men's faces and I've seen the other bits and pieces a few times.'

'And you've got Vic,' I reminded her.

'Yes,' she said quietly, 'I've got my Vic, bless his heart. He's a lot better now but that's not why I came in here this morning. Your sister-in-law rang to tell me she's worried about you. She wants to know how you are.'

'Oh,' I said, 'and how am I?'

Joan coloured. 'I heard you running your shower in the middle of the night and now you're walking around the flat with no clothes on. Perhaps you ought to be telling me how you are. Vic and I know you've been ill and we're desperately sorry about Sara. Finding her like that must have been a terrible shock.'

'It was a bit of a shock to walk into the bedroom and find a body,' I corrected her. 'You can report back to Delia and say I'm not terribly upset. I'm not trying to upset you either, Joan, but the truth is I only wanted the woman for one thing and thanks to her daughter, I wasn't getting much of that. So thank you for your interest and all that but I'd like to finish my breakfast and go to work, so if you don't mind.'

This time Joan's colour was higher. At the door, she turned and said, 'I'll tell you this, Michael Brent. Either you are more unbalanced than you know or you are the most callous bastard I have ever known. Sara was a lovely young woman and...'

'Fuck off!' I was shouting as I almost ran across the room to push her through the door, 'For Christ's sake will you just fuck off and leave me alone!'

I resisted the temptation to get back in the shower. I resisted the temptation to pour myself a drink. I resisted the temptation to let Crazy Bear off the leash and smash up the furniture. Instead I curled up on the bed and asked Margery why every woman I ever loved is dead. I wanted to know how I did it. The photograph told me nothing other than it needed dusting. 'Sod you,' I told it without meaning a word of it. 'All you ever wanted me for is fucking and the boys.'

I left the bedroom, poured myself a drink, swallowed it, replenished it, and asked Crazy Bear why all women care about in a man is fucking.

'Squaw not care who fuck,' Crazy Bear said, shaking his head gloomily. 'I tell you big truth. One time I sit round fire with horse trader and another brave. We drink, talk, trade, more drink, more talk. Horse trader go. I get up drunk, go in wrong teepee, fuck squaw and sleep. Next morning I come out of wrong teepee. Other brave come out of my teepee. I go in my teepee, sit on blanket and eat. Squaw say I snore terrible the whole night long, what wrong with me? I say what about fuck? Squaw says what about fuck? So I learn squaw don't care who fuck. Squaw only care who snore.'

'Hey,' I said, 'that's funny. That's really funny.' I had the half filled glass in my hand and was still laughing when the doorbell rang and I opened it to Sergeant Ginney and another man in plain clothes.

'Good morning, Mr Brent,' said Ginney, 'I expect you remember me. This is Detective Constable Harris. Do you mind if we come in?'

Chapter Sixteen

The doorbell rang again about a minute after the two policemen walked in and looked at the shit coloured wall paper before sitting opposite me. Harris heaved himself to his feet with a sigh and I heard him tell Delia that this was not a good time to call. No, he couldn't say quite when the interview would be finished. Why didn't she and my brother go home and wait to be contacted?

He closed the door on her questions and gave me a brief smile as he sat down again. 'Inquisitive lady, your sister-in-law, sir. You'll have to ask her to excuse me when you see her again.'

'Oh,' I said. 'I will be seeing her again then?'

'Is there any reason why you shouldn't, Mr Brent?'

'I thought you were here to arrest me.'

Ginney held up his hand and opened his notebook. 'There's no question of that at this time, Mr Brent. We're here to clear up one or two anomalies, that's all. In your statement in Mrs Leighton's flat, you told me that you and the deceased were good friends. Does that mean you had a sexual relationship?'

'Yes.'

'You also told me you thought Mrs Leighton was going away for a short holiday. No one else we spoke to seems to know anything about a holiday and that includes her employer. To the best of her husband's knowledge, all of her clothes are hanging in the wardrobe and her suitcase doesn't appear to have been touched. Can you tell me what made you think she was going away?'

'It was her husband who told me. He approached me in the church after my son's wedding and told me they were going away together.'

'In our interview with Mr Leighton, he said he was home all that day. According to him, he did not go to the church, nor did he attempt to contact you in any other way.'

'Then he's a bloody liar..'

I stopped as Ginney stared me down. 'Right now, Mr Brent, Constable Harris and I are merely trying to establish the truth. Nothing we say is meant to antagonize you and I strongly advise you not to get excited or upset. Understood?'

I nodded.

'Accepting for the moment that Mr Leighton did tell you they were going away together, how did you feel about it?'

'I didn't like it. I couldn't understand it but I really couldn't concentrate on what he was saying. My son had just got married, the photographer was calling me, and my wife wasn't there. I just had time to take the keys from him.'

'A moment, Mr Brent,' Ginney said. 'Your wife wasn't there?'

'My late wife.'

'I see.' He drew a deep breath and turned over a page in his notebook. 'Tell me, Mr Brent. Since you and Mrs Leighton were lovers, surely you had your own key to her flat?'

'It never came up. I couldn't just barge in when Julie was there. I only went to the flat when Sara and I were alone.'

'Apart from the day she was killed?'

'I told you, I went there to collect Julie's suitcase.'

'Another suitcase that had not been packed.' The two policemen exchanged glances and the much heavier Harris got to his feet and stood by the door as Ginney closed his notebook.

'It is my duty to tell you Mr Brent,' he said formally, 'that I am not satisfied with your answers to my questions. I would like to continue this interview at the station. Have you any objection to coming to the station with us?'

I shook my head.

'Would you like to contact your solicitor?'

I shook my head.

As we left the flat, I saw Joan's door open and Delia came on to the landing demanding to know what was going on.

The two policemen ignored her. I shook my head.

Inside the interview room, I was told by Ginney that I would be asked to make a voluntary statement because I was the first on the murder scene. It would be in my own interest to try to show that I was there as an innocent visitor about some legitimate business. If I had no objection my statement would be taped, copied, and I would be asked to sign it. If at any time, I wanted to halt the interview and ask for my solicitor to be present, I was free to do so. If at any time, I wanted to halt the interview and leave, I was free to do so. Meaning that at this time, I have not been charged with any misdemeanour. Did I understand?'

I nodded to show I understood and with some prompting from Ginney's notes, repeated everything I said in Sara's flat and everything I said in my own flat. I told them I was sure in my own mind that Paul Leighton had murdered his wife and tricked me into visiting the place. I said there was nothing more I could tell them except I was responsible for her death. Asked what I meant by that, I said if she hadn't got involved with me she would still be alive. Once more Sergeant Ginney asked me if I would like my solicitor to be present before I signed my statement. I shook my head, waited for my words to be copied, signed it, and to the accompaniment of Crazy Bear's howls of anguish, foot stamping, and breast beating, was formally charged with the murder of Sara Leighton.

A red eyed Bobby and a furious Delia, who'd been kept waiting by the front desk, were allowed a few minutes to tell me what a bloody fool I was and that they'd engaged a solicitor. I met Ian George for the first time the night after I was locked up on remand for psychiatric and medical reports and while further investigations were being carried out by the police. The frowning solicitor told me he had a copy of my statement and it had been very unwise of me to make it without his being there. I told him I expected it was unwise. But then, I wasn't accustomed to being interviewed in a police station and charged with murder.

'Quite so,' said George, 'and had I been present at the interview, you might not have been. The evidence is circumstantial and the case seems to rest on your statement and Mr Leighton's word against yours. But what's done is done. I think the sooner we employ silk the better. Have you heard of Arnold Plater?'

I had not and I regretted agreeing to employ him the moment I set eyes on the little fat man. He stood on the other side of the table, smoothed a few long hairs across his otherwise naked scalp, and said without preamble, 'Mr Brent, in your statement you say that you and Mrs Leighton were lovers.'

'We were.'

'Of course you were, Mr Brent, but I'd like you to be a little more specific. Were you friends? Did you go out together, hold hands on occasion and enjoy each other's company? Or was the woman just the occasional bit of cunt?'

Crazy Bear saw red. Whooping, he leapt on the table, raised his tomahawk high, and split the arrogant bastard in two. While he

98

gloried in his bloodletting, I leapt to my feet and pushed my chair back. As the prison warder at the door stiffened and Ian George put a restraining hand on my arm, Plater sat down quickly and chuckled.

'I'm afraid I'm not built for fisticuffs, Mr Brent,' he said, 'and let me tell you this. If you found that hard to deal with, wait until the prosecuting counsel gets going on you.' I slumped back in my chair and watched him hold out a fat little hand for the sheaf of papers in front of the solicitor. As he did so, Ian George opened his brief case and took out a neatly folded copy of *The Daily Mail*.

'Mr Brent,' he said quietly, 'I have to tell you that Mrs Leighton was buried yesterday morning at Mr Leighton's request. We could have asked for the body to be held during the course of the trial but since the Crown Prosecution and Mr Plater are in agreement as to the cause of death, the coroner saw no purpose in delaying the funeral.' He glanced at Plater who nodded his consent before the solicitor unfolded the paper and turned it towards me. Photographs of the dark suited and bare headed Paul Leighton, clutching his weeping daughter's hand in front of the flower bedecked coffin, were prominently featured on the front page. Below the photographs and continued on page three was the interview given exclusively to a *Daily Chronicle* reporter immediately after the burial was completed.

Mr Leighton, the obviously smitten lady reporter gushed, turned away from the grave fighting to control his emotion. As he brushed his fair hair back from his forehead, he said brokenly that he would have to be mother and father to his little daughter. Perhaps one day, Julie would get over her tragic loss but he never would. Yes, he admitted, when the question was put by our reporter, Sara and he were divorced. The fact his wife left him was due entirely to the evil influence of a third party who, he'd been told by the police, should not be named while enquiries were ongoing. All he could say was that his darling Sara was far too trusting for her own good. He blamed himself for being weak when she told him she was leaving him for another man. He believed her when she said she no longer loved him and that is what led to her death. If only he'd found the courage to fight for her love, she might have been alive today.

'It's a load of bollocks,' I said, crumpling the paper and pushing back across the table. 'He wasn't a good husband. She took Julie away because she hated him.'

'So what if she did?' asked Plater. 'It doesn't help your case.'

'But the bastard knocked her about,' I protested. 'Surely there's a record of that in their divorce proceedings. She was terrified of him.'

Plater shrugged his plump shoulders. 'Yet in your interview with the police, you said you thought they were going away together.'

'Because that was what he told me in the church,' I began and, suddenly remembering the nightmare in Sara's bedroom, said, 'He was there. In the flat. He hit me with something.'

Ian George exchanged a glance with Plater before giving me a hard stare and saying, 'That wasn't in your statement to the police.'

'I forgot. Besides, I didn't see him, I didn't get the chance. When I saw Sara was dead, I forgot everything else.'

Crazy Bear dropped the tomahawk he held and aped Plater's dismissive shake of the head. 'Since you can't prove who attacked you and it wasn't mentioned during the interview, I think that episode had best stay forgotten for the moment. In his statement, Mr Leighton told the police he has never been inside the flat and there is no reason to attack his credibility unless he is a suspect or he is giving evidence in the case. You are the man on trial, Mr Brent, and so far I have not been told that Mr Leighton will be called by the prosecution. Now sir, there is no need for the big guns yet. I am going to send a junior to represent you in the magistrate's court tomorrow. You will plead not guilty and he will ask for bail. Naturally, the police will object. In view of your statement in which, whatever you meant by it, you admit responsibility for Mrs Leighton's death – and it cannot be shown that you did not murder her – the police will have their way. Accept it, Mr Brent. You will be remanded in custody until the trial but casting doubts upon the veracity of your statement, and the circumstances in which it was made, will be a step in the right direction.'

The next morning, at the request of the police, I was given a further remand in custody for psychiatric reports while their own enquiries were completed and a date for the trial set. Before I was taken back to Brenton, Ian George came down to the holding cell to show me another copy of *The Daily Mail*. I read that Paul Leighton, who had given an exclusive interview to this newspaper after his murdered wife's funeral, aroused such a wave of sympathy from Mail readers he was now the slightly bemused recipient of several dozen cheques and eight proposals of marriage. When the package of letters was handed to him by our reporter, Mr Leighton smiled gently

100

and promised to reply to everyone as soon as he possibly could. Crazy Bear laughed like a drain all the way back to the cell.

The wing governor interviewed me and said since I'd be his guest for another two or three months, it might be useful if I had a trade. I told him I was a tailor's cutter and a factory manager. He laughed and offered me a job in the kitchens as soon as one became available. I said yes, anything to get me out of the cell. He laughed again and told me to borrow a library book for the time being, he'd see what he could do. Peeling potatoes and scrubbing pans must have been overcrowded professions in the kitchens of Brenton Prison. I had still heard nothing from the wing governor when, some weeks later, the prison doctor took my blood pressure for the second time. He said it was higher than it should be but in the circumstances, that was only to be expected. He listened to my chest, thumped my back, looked down my throat, and asked for a sample of urine. He told me that when my case came up he was to give the court a report on my physical and mental health. That was why I wasn't to try putting on an act. Acts wouldn't wash with him. He might be a doctor and involved in all that caring profession guff but he was also a hard man. He'd had years of experience seeing through remand prisoners who put on an act. Especially those murdering bastards who know exactly what they're doing while they're choking the life out of their victims but thirty seconds later, haven't the vaguest idea of why they did it.

'Oh yes,' he said while I got dressed and sat by his desk, 'I've had plenty of time to study customers of that sort, Mr Brent, so don't try any bullshit on me. Have you got the message?' I nodded to show I'd got the message. He asked if I'd been brought up in a normal family environment and how many brothers and sisters I had. When I said yes, normal mum, normal dad, and one normal brother, he wanted to know how I felt about women. I shrugged and he asked if I knew it was wrong to kill a woman whatever the provocation.

'Provocation?' I asked.

'Just suppose,' he asked confidentially as he moved his chair close enough for our knees to touch, 'a nice looking little prick teaser leads a fellow on and when he gets a hard on, she crosses her legs and laughs in his face. And just suppose he loses control and gives her a punch in the face or even grabs her by the throat and strangles her, it's only what the little bitch was asking for, wasn't it?'

101

'Was it?'

'Of course it was, we all know that. At the same time, we also know that killing is wrong. If it was you who killed the little prick teaser, you'd know you'd done wrong, wouldn't you?'

'The way I did wrong when I killed Margery?'

He raised his eyebrows and stared at me. 'Margery? Who is Margery?'

'My wife. My wife who died of cancer.'

'Oh, I see.' He scribbled an additional note on his pad. 'I didn't know about that. Tell me, Mr Brent, does the fact that your wife died of cancer make you resent other women in some way? Healthy women who had no right to be healthy while your wife was dying of cancer?'

Needing to get as far away from him as possible, I leaned back in my chair and said, 'I didn't resent Sara Leighton for being healthy, if that's what you're trying to make me say.'

He told me not to develop an attitude. An attitude wouldn't impress him, nor would it help me with my case. He put the note pad in a folder, put the folder in a desk drawer, turned the key in the lock, and ostentatiously tucked the key in his waistcoat pocket. Rubbing his hands together, he said there was something about me that interested him and he would very likely want to interview me again before the case came to trial. He didn't. The next time I saw him was three months later in court. He gave his medical opinion in a world weary voice obviously developed for court appearances. In answer to leading questions from the prosecuting counsel, he told the judge that I was physically strong enough to have committed the crime as described by the police. So far as my state of mind was concerned, there was some evidence of depression and self recrimination after my wife died, but I knew right from wrong and would be fully responsible for my actions.

The prison doctor was followed by police evidence stating that I had made a statement admitting responsibility for the death of Sara Leighton. A statement I had withdrawn after receiving advice from my solicitor. Plater, who had ignored the doctor's evidence, cross examined both police officers.

'No, my lord,' Sergeant Ginney said to the judge in answer to the barrister's first question, 'the accused was not arrested at his home.

He was asked to accompany me and another police officer to Nutting Street police station and make a voluntary statement.'

'Did he accompany you willingly?'

Ginney nodded his head. 'Yes, my lord.'

'Thank you sergeant. Was Mr Brent's solicitor present during the interview during which he allegedly confessed to the murder of Mrs Leighton?'

'No, my lord. The accused was reminded of his rights before we began the interview but prior to making his statement, he said he did not require the services of a solicitor.'

'Thank you.' Plater turned away, dropped his sheaf of papers on a table, and asked casually, 'Did you find it necessary to question the accused during the interview?'

Sergeant Ginney stared at the back of Plater's wig. 'Well of course we asked him questions.'

Plater turned back to face the sergeant. 'You did not remind the accused that he was there to make a voluntary statement and allow him to get on with it?'

'That's not how it's done,' Ginney replied incautiously. 'Besides, considering the state he was in, we'd have been there all night.'

'Considering the state he was in,' Plater repeated slowly. 'Would you mind explaining that remark. For the benefit of the court, of course.'

Ginney swallowed noisily. 'Mr Brent was rather nervous, that's all,' he backtracked. 'He was in a bit of a state.'

'Was he nervous and in a bit of state when you called on him earlier that day?'

'No, my lord.'

'Did he become nervous and in a bit of a state when you asked him to accompany you to the police station.'

'Not that I noticed, my lord.'

Plater pulled at his upper lip. 'Sergeant Ginney, you have told this court that the accused was perfectly calm, both at home and when he accompanied you to the police station. Are you now saying he became agitated in the interview room?'

'Well yes, my lord, I suppose I am.'

'Because you were hectoring him?'

'No, my lord, nothing of the kind,' Ginney told the judge. 'Detective Constable Harris and I did not hector Mr Brent at any time during the interview. We were merely trying to get to the truth of the matter.'

'Thank you, sergeant,' Plater said dryly. 'A truth you had already decided on, no doubt.' And just when I thought he had the arrogant bastard on the ropes, he said he had no further questions for the witness at this time.

He returned to the matter of my state of mind when Harris took the stand. Seemingly indifferent, he riffled through his notes and said, 'Tell me, constable. When you interviewed him, did the accused make a completely voluntary statement admitting responsibility for the death of Mrs Sara Leighton?'

'The prosecuting counsel looked up sharply when Harris smiled broadly and turned to face the judge. 'Oh no, my lord,' he said confidently, 'we had to get the truth out of him.'

'Why had to?' The words were like a whiplash and the smiled was wiped from Harris' face on the instant.

Turning back to Plater, he said hurriedly, 'It was a perfectly normal interview, sir. None of our questions were too difficult for the prisoner to answer and when he asked for his solicitor, we suspended the interview at once.'

'That was after he signed the statement, was it not?'

'Yes.'

'Quite so.' Plater paused for a moment and then said slowly and very distinctly, 'Constable Harris, I put it to you that Sergeant Ginney and you invited Mr Brent to accompany you to Nutting Street police station and make a voluntary statement. He was not in custody at that time and he went with you willingly. But the moment you had him there, you and Sergeant Ginney decided that your man was not going to leave that interview room without being charged with the murder of Mrs Leighton. Perhaps you had already decided on that course of action when you collected him from his home?'

Harris looked trapped but seized on the apparent loophole. 'No, not at that time sir. Not for certain.'

'I suggest that you had. I further suggest that you questioned Mr Brent in a manner designed to make him confess to a murder he later denied having committed.'

'No sir. We followed the correct procedure.'

'I see.' Plater moved closer to the witness box. 'Constable Harris, To be absolutely clear about this, I am going to ask you the question

I have already put to Sergeant Ginney. Having invited Mr Brent to make a voluntary statement, did you afford him the opportunity to do so?'

'I'm not sure I understand the question, sir.'

'I am asking if you allowed Mr Brent to say his piece without interruption before you began to question him?'

'Oh no sir. His statement was made in response to our questioning.'

'And if at any time he declined to answer or his answer did not accord with the facts as you understood them, did you persist in your questioning.'

'Well yes, we have to.'

'You persisted in your questioning,' repeated Plater. 'Thank you constable, that is precisely what I want the court to understand.' Plater turned to the judge and smiled. 'Thank you, my lord. I have no further questions for this witness at this time.'

John Hughes, the prosecuting counsel, held up his hand as the constable was about to step down. 'Tell me,' he asked, 'was the accused suspected of murdering Mrs Leighton when you took him to the police station?'

'Well yes sir. We thought he might be implicated in the murder.'

'Thank you, constable. Now tell me this. Would murder suspects normally be allowed to make a statement without interruption?'

'No sir, they would not.'

'Would any suspect, whatever crime he or she might be accused of committing, make a statement without interruption?'

'No sir.'

'But why not? As my learned friend has taken great pains to point out, the accused was invited to make a voluntary statement.'

Harris squared his shoulders and glared at Plater when he said, 'The questions are asked to make sense and order of what's being said.'

'To make sense and order of what's being said,' repeated Mr Hughes, also glancing at Arnold Plater. 'Thank you constable, that is precisely what I want the court to understand.'

The post mortem evidence was read out in a flat voice and not challenged. How could it be. Everyone in the country knew that Sara Leighton had been choked to death. It was in all the papers. Someone put his hands around her throat and pressed both thumbs hard into the windpipe. Someone looked into her face and squeezed until she could no longer breathe. Watching her terror. Did she make the sounds Margery made when she died? Had she made the same last reach for air? Finding none when she needed it most? Was she asking Michael, where are you, you lousy bastard? Like Margery must have been asking. Why wasn't I doing something while they were being slaughtered? I didn't know. How could I know?

The policeman sitting beside me in the dock nudged my elbow and we stood up to face the judge as he called for a lunch recess and left the court. I was still thinking of Margery when I taken down to the cell, the door locked behind me, and the policeman said through the hatch, 'It's no use feeling sorry for yourself now, you murdering bastard. You should have thought of all that before you did the poor cow in.'

I wiped my eyes and supposed he was right. I should have thought of all that before I killed Margery too.

I hardly touched my lunch. 'Bad conscience', muttered my friend the policeman, belching beer spray in my face while he escorted me up the stairs and into the courtroom. The prosecution rested. Before I was called to give evidence on my own behalf, Plater had Sergeant Ginney recalled to the witness box.

'One small point, sergeant,' the barrister said with an apologetic smile. 'When my learned friend, the prosecuting counsel, questioned you, you told the court the accused confessed to murder during the first interview you had with him.'

'Yes, my lord,' Ginney said stiffly. 'Later, he withdrew the confession on the advice of his solicitor.'

'Quite so,' said Plater, 'but tell me this, Sergeant Ginney. Did Mr Brent confess to killing Mrs Leighton or being responsible for her death?'

Ginney stared at the barrister. 'It's the same thing, ain't it?'

'No sergeant, it is not at all the same thing. But thank you. That will be all.'

The sergeant nodded and as he left the witness box, Plater turned to an usher and said quietly, 'Call Michael Brent.'

Chapter Seventeen

The constable and I rose to our feet like a pair of marionettes and marched shoulder to shoulder to the witness box. Standing to attention, I repeated the oath and, while Plater shuffled papers, took the opportunity to look around me. For the first time since the trial began, I had a full view of the court and everyone – jury, judge, and the public in the well – was staring back at me. Obviously, I'd been the centre of attention from the moment I was brought into the dock but until that moment, I hadn't been aware of the depth of feeling. I knew I was hated. The warder who'd told me to stop feeling sorry for myself and give some thought to what I did to that poor young woman, told me that. But he was only one man. When I was escorted into the dock at the beginning of the trial, I heard someone whisper 'you ought to swing for this you dirty shit bastard' but even that only made two. Now I could see it in all the faces turned toward me. Every one of them convinced they were looking at the murderer of Sara Leighton. I was unable to believe it. This stupid load of fuck-ups actually believed I was guilty of choking the life out of the only good thing that had happened to me since Margery died. They were crazy. As crazy as Crazy Bear – and where was he when I needed him? Nowhere. I knew he'd piss off once trouble came close to him. He was like the rest of the bastards. All over me on the good days. Crossing the road to get away from me on the bad days. Bastards, bastards, bastards.

'You are Michael Brent and you live at...' someone was saying for the second time. I looked at Plater in his wig and gown and, assuming he hated me as much as everybody else in the court did, said, 'Yes, who did you expect to be standing here?'

Someone sniggered, someone banged a hammer and told me to answer the questions put to me and not waste the court's time being facetious. I wanted to say I wasn't being facetious but Plater was asking me how long I'd known Sara Leighton and what was our relationship. I told him about Delia inviting her to my flat warming, our vegetarian lunches, our occasional trips out with her daughter Julie. I told him about the night Sara and I became lovers and about my sister-in-law's suggestion that Julie should become a bridesmaid at my son's wedding.

Plater stopped me by holding up his hand. 'The police have introduced evidence that seems to suggest you objected to Mrs Leighton's daughter Julie becoming a bridesmaid. According to the police, you objected so strongly you destroyed the dress made for her to wear. Why was that?'

I shook my head. 'I didn't object to Julie being a bridesmaid. The child hated the dress. I had another one made for her by a friend of mine.'

'Nevertheless, Mr Brent, I will be calling a witness who has made a sworn statement that flatly contradicts that answer. Allow me to press you on the point. Are you telling this court the only reason you had a new dress made for Julie was because the child did not like the original dress?'

'Yes I am. That was the only reason.'

'Thank you Mr Brent. Did you murder Sara Leighton?'

'No, of course I didn't murder her. I found her dead and called the police.'

'What were your feelings when you found Mrs Leighton dead?'

'At first, I thought she was sleeping and touched her. I was very shocked when I realised she was dead. I think I fainted.'

'And vomited on the bedroom floor, I understand.'

'Yes.'

'Mr Brent, why did you say in your statement to the police that you were responsible for Sara Leighton's death?'

'I knew her husband didn't like me. I thought he may have killed her because of her relationship with me.'

Plater looked at the prosecuting counsel who returned a slight shake of the head. Turning back to me, he said mildly, 'Be that as it may, Mr Brent. Now sir, you have admitted to drinking heavily at your son's wedding reception. Can you account for your actions from the time you left the reception to the time you found Mrs Leighton's body?'

I told the judge I drove home with my son Dicky and my neighbours, Vic and Joan. I said that Dicky spent the night with me and the following morning his grandparents came to collect him for their return journey. After they had a coffee and left, I took the clothes George, Dicky, and I wore at the wedding back to Moss Brothers. Then I went to Sara's flat and found her dead.

When I finished, Plater nodded at the prosecuting counsel, thanked me, and sat down.

John Hughes got slowly to his feet. 'Mr Brent,' he said, 'I understand the police took the clothes you were wearing when you claimed to have discovered the body of Sara Leighton?'

'Yes but there was nothing on them.'

'Quite so,' Hughes agreed. 'Now sir, if we are to believe your story, we have to accept that you entered the premises where you found Mrs Leighton's body in the bedroom. You then collapsed on the floor, vomited, and fainted away. All without a mark on your clothing or your shoes to indicate that any of these things really happened.?'

'It is what happened. What else can I say?'

Hughes smiled bleakly. 'Quite a lot, I suspect, Mr Brent. Now sir, since you have admitted having a lot to drink the night before the murder, there is a possibility that your memory of the events might be impaired. I would therefore like to suggest a different scenario. I suggest that you visited Mrs Leighton's home twice on the morning she died. I further suggest that on the first occasion you visited the flat, you were wearing the suit you hired from Moss Brothers.'

I stared at him. 'No, of course I wasn't wearing the hired suit. Why on earth would I? I was taking the clothes back.'

'I am suggesting you wore the clothes because you went to the flat with the intention of murdering Mrs Leighton.'

'No, it's not true.'

'I put it to you, Michael Brent, that you took a change of clothing with you. You cruelly murdered Mrs Leighton, changed into your own clothes and returned the hired clothing; knowing that once returned to Moss Brothers, the shirts would be laundered and the suits steamed and pressed and returned to stock. Thus removing any possibility of forensic evidence against you.'

I shook my head. 'It was nothing like that. I took the clothes back before I went to the flat and found Sara.'

Hughes stepped closer to the witness box. 'I put it to you, Michael Brent, that wanting to be revenged on the woman you felt had turned her back on you, you committed a calculated, premeditated murder.'

'No.'

'I believe that you did, Mr Brent. And after returning the soiled garments, you returned to the flat and acted out your little charade for the benefit of the police.'

'If I had done that, what possible reason would I have for going back to the flat? There'd be no point.'

'But there would be a point, Mr Brent. Knowing that your connection with the deceased would be discovered when the body was found, what better way to protest your innocence than by pretending to find the body yourself?'

'I protested my innocence because I am innocent. I did not kill Sara Leighton.'

'That will be for the jury to decide, Mr Brent,' Hughes said with a nod in their general direction. 'Tell me this. From whom did you get the front door key to Mrs Leighton's flat?'

'I've already told you. Her husband gave it to me.'

'Her estranged husband?'

'Of course they were estranged. They were divorced, weren't they?'

'You have said on oath that Mr Leighton did not like you. Do you know this to be a fact?'

'Of course he didn't like me. He'd taken it into his head that I stole his wife.'

'Quite so, Mr Brent,' Hughes interrupted smoothly. 'Of course he did not like you. Yet you are asking the court to believe that this estranged husband who did not like you gave you the key to his ex-wife's flat? I suggest that you are lying. Mrs Leighton gave you the key so that you could visit her at will, didn't she?'

'No, she did not. Paul Leighton gave me the key in church after my son's wedding. He told me that he and Sara were reconciled. They were going to take a short holiday together and he asked me to collect Julie's clothes.'

'I put it to you that nothing of the sort happened and your story of meeting Paul Leighton in church or anywhere else on the day of your son's wedding is a complete fabrication. Mrs Leighton gave you the key to her home. She trusted you and you betrayed her trust in the cruellest way imaginable. You concocted the story about the Leightons' reconciliation so that your sister-in-law would take Julie Leighton home with her. After which, you drove to Mrs Leighton's

110

flat and let yourself in with every intention of murdering her. That is how it was, wasn't it, Mr Brent?'

'No, it was nothing like that.'

'Oh but I think it was, Mr Brent. I think that is exactly how it was.'

It wasn't a question and as Hughes gathered his robe round him and sat down, Arnold Plater bobbed up. 'Mr Brent, since the point has been raised, do you not think it odd that Paul Leighton, who you say did not like your relationship with his ex-wife, would give you the key to her flat?'

'In retrospect I do. On the day, I was thinking more about my son George's wedding and the fact that my late wife wasn't there to share it with me. When Paul Leighton handed me the key and said that he and Sara were going away for a few days, I simply took his word for it.'

'Thank you, Mr Brent. That is all I have for you at this time.'

The judge, after reminding me that I remained under oath and might be recalled, told my escort to return me to the dock.

'Call Paul Leighton,' said Plater. I watched as Paul, dressed in a dark grey suit and with his fair hair brushed back, entered the witness box and took the oath, looking anywhere but at me.

'Mr Leighton,' Plater said almost conversationally, 'I have the court's permission to treat you as a hostile witness. Do you understand what that means?'

'Yes thank you,' Paul answered politely. 'I know it's your duty to do the best you can for the accused.'

'Quite so. And you understand the oath you have just taken?'

'Oh I'll tell the truth all right. The truth doesn't frighten me. He's the one who's afraid of the truth coming out.'

'He, Mr Leighton?'

'Brent,' Paul spat. 'The man who murdered my wife.'

Plater waited for the hubbub to die down. 'Ex-wife surely, Mr Leighton?'

'That was his fault too,' Paul said bitterly. 'She would never had left me if he hadn't persuaded her to.'

'Really?' Arnold Plater paused to glance at his notes. 'Mr Leighton, Michael Brent has stated in this court that he first met Mrs Leighton at his flat warming, some eight months after your and your late ex-wife's divorce was finalized. Are you saying Mr Brent was lying about the date of their first meeting?'

'Of course he was lying. I was a good husband. We had a nice home and a beautiful little daughter. Why would she give all that up if it wasn't for him?'

Plater smiled and adjusted his wig. 'You really shouldn't ask me questions, Mr Leighton, but since you have, allow me to suggest a reason. Will you look at this photograph, please. It formed part of the evidence given in your divorce proceedings.' Prosecuting counsel got to his feet and Plater immediately gave way.

'Is this line of questioning relevant, my lord?' asked Mr Hughes. 'Mr Leighton is not on trial.'

'Mr Plater?' asked the judge.

'I am not impugning Mr Leighton's character, my lord,' Arnold Plater said mildly. 'Having been allowed to read the statement he made to the police, I merely question his recollection of certain events beginning with his relationship with his late wife as detailed in their divorce proceedings. Defence maintains that Mr Brent is telling the truth when he says he met Mrs Leighton for the first time at his flat warming and had no part in the divorce.'

'Very well.'

Plater bowed. 'Thank you, my lord.' Turning back to face Paul Leighton, he said, 'This photograph was part of the medical evidence proving that you beat your wife so severely she needed medical attention. I understand from the case records that you did so on more than one occasion. The deposition claimed physical and mental cruelty and those are the grounds on which the decree was granted. Unless I am mistaken, Mr Leighton, there was no mention of Michael Brent or any other third party during the proceedings?'

Paul reddened. 'My wife had a delicate skin,' he said grudgingly. 'She bruised easily. She only had to knock her arm against a chair or a door and she was black and blue for days. I said so at the time.'

'So you did, Mr Leighton. You were bitterly opposed to the divorce yet you did not name Mr Brent as the reason for your wife's desertion. Why was that?'

'I didn't know his name until I saw him come out of her flat.'

'I see.' Plater turned back to his notes. 'Mr Leighton, as my learned friend the prosecuting counsel rightly says, you are not on

112

trial and I urge you to consider your reply to my next question. Did you not tell the police that you have never visited your late wife?'

Paul's colour deepened. 'I never did. I knew the address and on the one occasion I meant to visit my wife, I saw Brent leaving and went away.'

'I see. Then I take it you had no knowledge of Mr Brent's involvement with Mrs Leighton at the time of your divorce?'

'I knew it was someone.'

'But not Mr Brent?'

'Not at the time, no.'

'Not at any time, Mr Leighton. Now then sir, your daughter visited you regularly, did she not? There was a court order to that effect.'

'She didn't come as often as I would have liked.'

'But she visited you regularly?'

'She did.'

'Did she have a key to her mother's flat?'

'Is that why you brought me here?' Paul shouted. 'To try to get a murderer off?'

Mr Justice Roberts quelled the hubbub with a rap of his gavel and glared at Paul Leighton. 'You are brought here to help us arrive at the truth in this matter,' he said distinctly.

Paul struck the edge of the witness box with a clenched fist. 'The truth is he murdered her!' he shouted again. 'I had to look at her body. How do expect me to feel...'

Another rap stopped him dead. 'The truth, Mr Leighton, is that you are guilty of contempt and that I will not tolerate in my court. Take him down. The court will recess for one hour.'

An apparently subdued Paul Leighton apologised for his outburst when he returned to the witness box and it seemed that the episode had taken the wind out of Plater's sails too. When Paul flatly denied giving me a key to Sara's flat and swore he had not been in the church or anywhere in its vicinity on the day of George and Donna's wedding, Plater merely thanked him. Hughes shook his head at the unspoken offer to cross examine and the judge, after a short lecture on the behaviour expected of witnesses, said he could go.'

'Go where?' Paul whined in much the manner he once asked me the same question. 'Where do you want me to go? He took away my wife. He made her stop loving me. I loved her...'

Mr Justice Roberts signalled to one of the policemen standing at the back of the court. 'This is not a matter for me...' he began but Paul was sobbing and coming at me screaming, 'You stole her from me, you bastard. You ought to swing...'

'But I didn't kill her,' I was on my feet and shouting back at him when two policemen grabbed Paul and dragged him away as my escort clapped a hand over my mouth and forced me back in my seat.

Paul and I having effectively closed the proceedings for the day, it was the following morning when the judge asked the jury, so far as they possibly could, to put Mr Leighton's unfortunate outburst out of their minds. Their duty was to concentrate only on the evidence and the closing arguments. He then asked Arnold Plater if he intended to call any more witnesses. When Plater got to his feet and said he had concluded the case for the defence, Hughes was invited to address the jury.

The counsel bowed and turned to face the jury. 'Ladies and gentlemen,' he began quietly, 'it is the function of the prosecution to prove the case against the accused. Since it is proof we are after and not conjecture, let us see what we have. We know that Mr Brent had been drinking heavily and as a pointer to his state of mind, we also know he annoyed several guests at his son's wedding reception. We know he was in the flat where the murder took place. In a statement given to the police he admitted responsibility for Mrs Leighton's death. Doctor Patel, in his evidence, said that when he was called out by a neighbour, he found Mr Brent depressed but not in his view, clinically so. Because Mr Brent had complained of sleeping badly, sedatives were prescribed but so far as he knew, not taken.'

Hughes pursed his lips and began to read from his notes. 'The doctor who examined him in prison agrees that Mr Brent was depressed. When questioned by me, he added that he examined Mr Brent both physically and in his state of mind. In his view there was nothing to suggest that Mr Brent is not capable of committing murder. Lastly, ladies and gentlemen, so far as a third party is concerned. Exhaustive enquiries have been carried out. No one other than the accused is known to have entered or to have left the flat during the hours medical evidence shows that the murder was committed. Michael Brent went to the flat to visit his ex-lover. He was angry. He was drunk. He killed her. Coldly or in a rage only he knows, but he killed her. There is no other possible explanation of the facts placed before you and I ask you to find Michael Brent guilty of the murder of Mrs Sara Leighton.

Hughes sat down and his place was taken by Plater who said, equally without histrionics, 'There are two vital pieces of evidence against Michael Brent. First, the opportunity. Undeniably he was in the flat and had Mrs Leighton been alive when he got there, he had every opportunity to commit murder. It is Mr Brent's contention that Mrs Leighton was not alive when he entered the flat and nothing has been produced in evidence to prove him wrong. Secondly we come to the question of the key. The counsel for the prosecution has made much of the supposed fact that Mr Leighton would not have given his estranged wife's lover a key to the front door of her flat. I say he would and for reasons of his own, he did exactly that. I will not attempt to make capital out of Mr Leighton's unfortunate outburst in court. That gentleman has been under much strain. I will say only this. Mr Brent swears he was approached by Mr Leighton, handed the key to the flat with the instruction to collect his daughter's suitcase, and that is what he attempted to do. Nothing has been proved to the contrary and beyond that point, all is supposition. Ladies and gentlemen, I ask you to accept Mr Brent's version of the events. He went to Mrs Leighton's flat to find a suitcase and found a body. When he was sufficiently recovered from the shock, he informed the police. That is all he did. Thank you.'

'You have heard arguments from both counsels,' Mr Justice Roberts told the jury, 'and effective arguments they were. The defence says much has been made of from whom Mr Brent acquired the key to the victim's home, the suggestion being that another party might be culpable. Since only one person is on trial here, I suggest that you disregard that issue. The fact is that no one other than Mr Brent has been shown to have visited Mrs Leighton's home on that morning. The defence claims that Mrs Leighton was dead when Mr Brent got there. On finding her body, he called the police. Nothing given in evidence disproves that statement. On the other hand, the prosecution says that Mr Brent took advantage of the opportunity to wear a hired suit of clothes when he visited the flat and found Mrs Leighton alive. There, says the Crown, an altercation took place. After which, he murdered her, changed his clothes, and returned the suit with any incriminating evidence that may have been clinging to it, to the hirers. When he arrived back at the flat, he induced a bout of sickness and called the police. All of which, it has to be said, is highly speculative. You, ladies and gentlemen of the jury, have seen Mr Brent on the witness stand and in the dock. It is for you to decide whether or not he carried out the murder by manual strangulation of Sara Leighton. If you decide that he did commit murder, he is guilty as charged. If your opinion is that he did not commit murder or that the evidence is not strong enough to prove the case against him, it will become your duty to acquit. Please go now and consider your verdict.'

Chapter Eighteen

Left to myself in the holding cell below the court, I sighed without knowing I'd held my breath, sat on the edge of the cot, and mourned for Sara. Or Margery. Or me. I didn't know which. Above me in the court, everyone who stared their hatred at me condemned me as a murderer. Every one of them convinced that I had created that twisted dead thing out of my lover's living body. I felt their sympathy reach out to the red eyed Paul Leighton when he howled at Plater, 'Is that why you brought me here? To try to get a murderer off?' And again when he asked the judge where he wanted him to go now that I'd murdered his wife. All right, the old boy choked him off but if the death penalty hadn't been abolished there was nothing the mob who watched Paul's performance would like better than see me strung up for murder.

My eyes too were wet when I looked up to see Crazy Bear sitting quietly beside me. 'And you can piss off too,' I told him. 'Who the hell needs you now?'

He rose to his feet, towered above me and folded his arms. 'You fight your own war in court room, Michael Brent,' he said simply. 'Crazy Bear no use in witness box.'

I shrugged. 'I wasn't fighting. I was answering their bloody questions, I can't even remember what I said.'

'You fight well,' he replied. 'Crazy Bear say you fight well and win.'

'In a pig's eye I won,' I said, aiming a slap at his bare backside. 'Those bastards up there want to see me hanging from a rope.'

He caught my hand and laughed. 'You crazy like Apache, Michael Brent. You not hang for crows to peck.'

'From your mouth to God's ears,' I replied and despite the best efforts of the prosecuting counsel, God must have heard.

After the not guilty verdict, which had more to do with Paul Leighton's outburst on the witness stand than anything I said or did to protect myself, I slumped back on the bench. The noises in my head began to reverberate and swell against the sudden babble and rush of people standing, stretching, and scurrying past me towards the opened doors of the courtroom. Other people stopped in front of me but my eyes had misted over and I could not see them properly.

I heard Arnold Plater congratulate me as he shook my hand and clapped me on the shoulder. I could feel his excitement when he said we'd done bloody well, my lad, bloody well. His voice faded and moved back through the haze and it was Delia and Bobby's turn to hug me and for Delia to tell me I was much too thin, it must have been the prison food, and I needed fattening up.

When I broke free of her, Ian George took my hand in both of his and to my surprise, I saw he too was crying. He told me the street outside was full of photographers and reporters. They were waiting outside the flat too, something Joan and Vic weren't going to thank me for. While I was trying to remember who the hell Joan and Vic were, he handed me my credit cards and some cash and suggested I lay low in a hotel for a few weeks. Another factor was that Paul Leighton and his daughter had disappeared but not before he uttered threats against me and while I took that in, Arnold Plater swam back through the mist to tell me that he was more accustomed to being threatened than I would ever be. If I took his advice, I wouldn't give Leighton and his threats another thought. He patted my shoulder again and said, 'Do as Ian tells you, Michael my friend. Just go away. Put it behind you and go somewhere you can sleep, eat, and relax for a few weeks.'

Quite suddenly, I felt cold as ice. Reacting more than I thought I could to the verdict, I tried to say, 'That sounds good. I need a rest. But please get me out of here.'

What came out was an incoherent stammer and Delia, seeing me trembling, took charge. I was glad of the support of her arm through mine as we ran the gauntlet of photographers and jostling reporters wanting me to comment on Paul Leighton's threats and tell the world about my future plans. My future plans? A few hours earlier, I hadn't known I had a future to plan for. I shook my head dumbly at a man who pushed a microphone in my face and climbed into the waiting taxi. Bobby told the driver to take us to the Madden Road and to hell with the photographers who continued to stand round the cab, popping their flash guns in our eyes. Inevitably we were followed and had to put up with another barrage of questions and cameras when we reached the house. We walked through it to the door, Delia drowning out the chattering voices by talking nineteen to the dozen. In the welter of words I heard her say she had a meal waiting because she knew I was going to be acquitted and no one was going to

118

deprive her of the pleasure of feeding her brother-in-law, darling. I thanked her and sat at the table.

After the grunge I'd eaten in prison, the food she put before me looked wonderful and smelled better. I sniffed at it, excused myself, and went into the bog. Bobby knocked after a while and I came out wiping my eyes. I tried to tell him I was sorry, I could see how much trouble he and Delia had been to, but I couldn't eat. I just needed to lie down for a while and then I'd be all right. When I got into the spare bedroom I saw a tray of sandwiches and a flask of coffee on the bedside cabinet. With difficulty, I resisted Crazy Bear's urge to throw it all through the closed window and flopped face down on the bed. To sleep. To dream. Of Sara or Margery. Margery or Sara, I didn't know which. I could see she was dead. Her eyes and mouth were open. Her lips drawn back in a scream of silent agony. I'd done nothing to help her when she needed me most. Whichever. Either. Both. Whichever. Either. Both. I woke up thinking of a woman in a past life who sold shoes in a shop on a roundabout. She got up from a chair and held out her arms to me as I entered the shop. She was begging me not to cry.

My photograph, 'the most distorted they could find out of all the photographs they took, darling, and you don't look a bit like that, not really,' insisted Delia as though I cared a shit, graced the front pages of all the next morning's newspapers, mostly under the banner headline 'ACQUITTED'. It seemed that no one could have been more astonished by the irrationality of juries than the leader writer of one of the tabloids. While listing with shock and horror some of the other felons who had escaped their deserved fate through the vagaries of twelve good men and true, he or she skated round the law of libel by keeping any direct reference to me off the leader page. After breakfast, Bobby and I shouldered our way through the remaining representatives of the freedom of the press and drove to the flat to pack a suitcase and pick up my car.

After he squeezed my arm and left me at the door, I stepped over the letters on the mat, threw a few clothes into a holdall Dicky once left behind and, deciding not to bother Joan and Vic with my problems, got in the car and drove to Winchester for no other reason than I like the name. I booked into a small hotel and, after telling the receptionist I was recovering from an operation, spent the following week in my room, eating, sleeping, watching telly, and starting to grow a beard. At the end of the week, no longer able to take the isolation, I ventured out in daylight and chanced going into a pub. No one, including the barman I had to ask three times for a pint, paid the slightest attention to me. I walked back to the hotel, had a couple of jars at the bar, and telephoned Bobby. He said the newspapers seemed to have forgotten me but even if they did start sniffing round when I got back, they had to get over it sometime. Besides, I was needed at the factory. I drove back to the flat, opened a bottle, and returned to the factory the following morning.

Two newspapers, both claiming exclusives, reported that I had been seen entering the factory through a half hidden side gate we didn't have. The chief crime reporter of one was pleased to tell his avidly admiring public that he recognized me at once, despite the obviously false beard I was sporting. But then, he wrote, he'd had many years tracking down men with something to hide. I rang Ian George but he said it was too much of a generalization to sue, I didn't need the publicity, and since there was no sign of Paul Leighton, they'd soon decide I wasn't much of a story any more.

Work helped at first, despite the way everybody treated me with kid gloves. In every other way, I was back to square one. When poor old Vic took ill again and Joan sent for an ambulance rather than ask me for help, that was it. I had acquired another bunch of neighbours who crossed the road when they saw me coming. At this rate, half London took to the hills at my approach. Not that I cared. I didn't give a sod. I had Crazy Bear to drink with. Crazy Bear, who was developing a healthy beer gut, didn't give a sod who heard him fart, and rolled into work whenever he felt like it. Then I drove into the back of a bus that had stopped at a pedestrian crossing and got myself spread all over the papers again.

That evening, Bobby came up to the flat and said he couldn't carry on like this. God alone knew what I was doing to myself but I was driving him mad. He offered to buy me out so naturally I tried to solve the problem in the only way I knew. And for the first time either of us could remember, my brother brushed aside my clumsy attempt at a punch at his jaw and knocked me cold.

The next morning I asked for tranquillizers. Dr Patel prescribed a rest, preferably with a change of scene that involved more than a room in a cheap hotel and a bar in a pub. He said I'd gone back to work too soon. In my state of mind, I was unable to cope with pressure and my drinking was making the situation worse.

'Come on, doc,' I said, 'you can see I'm ill. I can't stop my bloody hands shaking.'

Patel shook his head. 'Tranquillizers are no use to you, Mr Brent. If you want a cure for your self-inflicted wounds, forget the whiskey bottle and get out into the fresh air. Start using your two legs.'

I told him he was a lousy doctor. Patel laughed and said he probably was. I told him if he knew the first thing about his English patients, he'd know when one of them is ill and needs treatment. He said some of his Asian patients get pissed too and he didn't give them tranquillizers. Hadn't I heard of puggle pani? I told him to get the hell out of my home. He laughed and went. Bobby came half an hour later. After I asked him where he'd learned to punch so hard and he said I'd taught him, I told him how Patel said I should cure myself.

'There's no need to talk about buying me out yet,' I said, 'I've still got some money left over from the house sale. If it's all right with you, I'd like to take some time off. Suppose you get a manager in and let's see how I am in a few months. I'm no good to you now.'

'Keep in touch,' Bobby said as he put an arm round my shoulders, 'I'll miss you, you rotten sod.'

I didn't say yes you'll miss me like a hole in the head or not if you buy yourself a punch bag or any of the other smart arse remarks that occurred to me because Bobby kissed my cheek before he left and I wanted to cry too. Before I did, I packed a couple of bags, put a key through Joan and Vic's door with a note to say I'd be away for a few weeks, and because it was a sunny day, drove to Bournemouth. I booked into a hotel and said again to the receptionist that I'd come to recuperate after an illness. After she insisted on carrying my bags up to the room and told me I couldn't have found a healthier spot, I got into bed, tucked my shaking hands and stumbling legs under the duvet. The next morning, I woke up sober enough to fancy and eat at least half of a full English breakfast.

On the beach, I met a girl who made perfect sense. She dropped a towel beside my deckchair and sat on it cross-legged while she took off her bikini top and draped it across my thigh. She said her name was Sandra and would I be interested in doing a little friendly business for thirty quid? I walked behind her to her flat and enjoyed

121

the way her near naked bottom wiggled as she climbed the stairs. In bed she was nothing special and neither was I but the sex and the feel of her body tucking neatly into mine made me feel better than I had in months. Better than better.

While we shagged and I heard Crazy Bear whooping his approval round the bed, I felt great. This was how fucking should be. No committal. No kissing. No talking about who or what we were. No disease. No relatives. Just a straightforward 'there's a French letter in the drawer by the bed lover, do you need any help putting it on' slap and tickle, without any risk brought on by contamination or prolonged association. We didn't know each other. We didn't want to know each other. If I saw her again, I probably wouldn't recognize her. Most likely, Sandra wasn't her real name. Just having it off with a prostitute for not too much money and why hadn't I thought of it before?

Crazy Bear said that all I needed was a bit of cunt and as usual, the big guy was right. Fuck'em and forget'em. Whip it in, whip it out, and wipe it. Wham, bam, thank you ma'am. That's what your dangly bit was given to you for. Enjoy it. I walked into the first restaurant I saw, ate the best lunch I'd eaten in weeks and spent the rest of the day on the beach, bathed in the warm glow of having had sex for its own sake.

That night, I saw Sandra again in the Winter Gardens. She had a man on her arm and she winked at me as she walked him by so he could follow her up the stairs to her flat and enjoy uncomplicated 'there's a French letter in the drawer lover' sex. So what did I expect for Christ's sake? She was a tart with her living to earn, wasn't she? Even so, seeing her with someone else put a damper on the evening. I walked back to the hotel reminding myself that fucking was something women did too. Sara had shagged other men before I knew her. Even Margery wasn't a virgin when we first made love. Not that I'd have known the difference if she hadn't told me because, although I would have been ashamed to admit it at the time, I was as pure in body as a dirty mind could get.

I walked into the hotel bedroom thinking of Margery. I'd brought her photograph with me and put it on the bedside cabinet when I unpacked and left my pyjamas on the bed. Someone had moved them. They'd turned down the bed, left the pyjamas under the pillow, picked up the photograph, dusted it, and put it down in a different

122

place. It was a complex frame. I'd never managed to dust its nips and tucks properly but that wasn't the point. Margery was mine and whoever touched her should have kept their dirty hands to themselves. For a moment I thought about ringing down to the desk and telling whoever answered that farting about with my wife's photograph wasn't included in the service I required but the throb in my head was threatening to come back so I told myself to forget it. Instead I poured a drink and lay on the bed, the memory of Sandra's thonged and rosy backside wiggling up the stairs before me giving me an erection.

Crazy Bear laughed. 'What you do with that, Michael Brent?'

'Make love to my hand,' I said, 'unless you want to do it for me.'

'Squaw work,' he told me and I said there was nothing wrong with a spot of DIY. Especially if it helped you forget that people have a habit of driving you to drink and doing crazy things.

Sandra dropped her towel on the beach and sat beside me the next day. I stiffened a little and she said, 'Relax lover, I'm on my lunch break. Care for a sandwich?' I propped myself up on an elbow and looked at her while we shared her ham and lettuce rolls. She was young but not too young. Pretty but not too pretty. After a few moments, she put her head on one side and returned the scrutiny.

'You're not going to give me any of that what's a nice girl like you crap, are you lover?' she asked.

I looked at the fine dusting of sand on her long tawny legs and grinned at her. 'To tell the truth, Sandra, I was thinking of when rather than what.'

She laughed back at me. 'Not on my full stomach, you're not. Besides, I wouldn't want you running out of money too soon and having to go back to the wife and kids.'

'The kids are all grown up,' I said, 'and my wife died of cancer five years ago. I'm all yours if you want me.' Surprised at how easily I could tell a stranger that Margery was dead, I missed Sandra's reply but I felt the pressure of her hand on my arm.

'Hey,' I said a little shakily, 'what's a nice girl like you...' and the pressure of her hand increased.

The sun was high, the breeze was light. We linked hands and dozed on our towels for an hour before going up to her room. This time the sex was better, for me anyway. Sandra was good natured enough to kid me along but we'd been closer to each other on the beach than we were in bed and we both knew it. And we both knew it wouldn't do to get too fond of each other. After I dressed, I lowered the duvet to caress her bare shoulders, drop a kiss on the end of her nose, and tell her I was leaving.

She smiled up into my eyes and said, 'So long, lover. Maybe I'll see you again one of these days.'

'Maybe,' I agreed as I closed her flat door behind me and drove back to my hotel..

Next morning I sent Bobby and Delia a postcard, telling them I was moving on to Brighton and would be staying at the Castle Hotel in case they wanted to send on any post. In fact they sent Sergeant Ginney.

I hardly had time to be shocked before he walked into my room, held out a hand and said, 'Bit of luck finding you so quickly, Mr Brent. I take it that's your late wife? She was very beautiful. Have you been reading the London newspapers?'

I ignored the hand and shook my head.

'Then you won't have heard that Mr Plater was attacked and seriously injured last week.'

I shook my head again and sat down.

'No,' said Ginney. 'Of course you haven't. Look, Mr Brent, when you were charged and brought to trial, I was a copper doing a job and the fact I thought you were guilty had as much to do with your woolly minded attitude as the evidence. It turns out I was completely off beam and I'm sorry. Why not let bygones be bygones and come down to the bar and have a drink. I'd best bring you up to date.'

Bringing me up to date meant telling me that Paul Leighton's erratic behaviour during the trial had been noted and the information passed on to Social Services who sent a young officer to speak to him and assess his daughter's situation. She didn't get past the door the first time she called, the second time he became abusive, and the third time he made the mistake of punching her and was arrested ten minutes later.

'Julie?' I asked.

'In care, Mr Brent. She may not be too happy but she is safe.'

'Does Delia know? She's fond of the child. We all are.'

'I'm sure you are but for now anyway, we are keeping her whereabouts secret.'

I finished my drink and refused another. 'For now?'

'While her father is at large. He told the tale to some smart-arsed magistrate who thought he'd suffered enough losing his wife and daughter. The silly sod tore into the social services department, apologised to Leighton for not being able to return his daughter and gave him probation. Leighton disappeared until last week when he grabbed Arnold Plater outside his apartment block and demanded to know your whereabouts. Plater told him to go to Hell and got badly beaten for his pains.'

'Plater once told me he wasn't built for fisticuffs,' I said, remembering the first time I met the plump little man. 'Is he badly hurt?'

'Nothing life-threatening but he's still in St George's under police guard. Leighton next called on your sister-in-law and pushed his way into her house. A card you sent from Bournemouth was on the mantelpiece and we're pretty sure he followed you there. If he spotted you, he may have gone to your hotel and found you'd gone. He might even have seen you with someone…'

'Sandra!' I said loudly enough to make heads turn. 'He could have seen me with Sandra. Who knows what he might be doing to her.'

As Ginney took out his notebook, I grabbed him by the sleeve. 'Not that bloody thing again. Sandra's a tart. If he spoke to her, she'd think he was a pick up and take him to her room. The bastard might be doing anything.'

'Her surname?' snapped Ginney, 'her address?'

I didn't know either. I began to stammer through the sudden rush of noise.

'Can you take me there?' Ginney cut in before rushing me out to his car. While he drove he handed me his mobile phone, gave me the number, and I found myself trying to describe Sandra.

'Not her nice smile, for fuck's sake,' Ginney growled as he swung out on the main road. 'Tell the bugger the colour of her hair, what she was wearing, and what direction she took you in when you left the fucking beach.' I passed on what he told me to a policeman who seemed to know the local girls well enough to be pretty sure who and where she might be.

'Ask him if he's got the all stations on Paul Leighton,' bellowed Ginney.

'Tell him the bugger's got it,' said the policeman. 'We're on the case.'

When we arrived at Sandra's home, we were waved on along the street by a Special who wouldn't take no for an answer, not even from Ginney. As he was pulling into the first parking bay he saw, I was out of the car and running back when the Special grabbed me and flattened me against the wall.

'They're coming up the street, you silly sod,' he said urgently. 'Don't spoil it now. We've got him.'

I looked over his shoulder and saw Sandra, her arm crooked in Paul's. She was wearing her bikini, smiling up at him the way she smiled up at me, wiggling the way she wiggled for me, and I hadn't realised how small she was. Or how bloody vulnerable. Sensing, rather than seeing me start to move, Ginney grabbed my arm.

'Believe me,' he said quietly, 'we're better at it and unless we catch him in the act, it's no go. Stay here with the constable and trust me.'

The two or three minutes I waited before the scream and the crash that had me halfway up the stairs and meeting Paul face to face seemed to last forever. He tried to stop and kick out at me but lost his footing and tumbled. Leaving him to the Special who came panting into the house behind me, I ran into the room and found a white faced Ginney unconscious on the floor and Sandra sitting on the bed, nursing her throat.

An instant later, she was in my arms, nuzzling her head in my jacket, and whispering huskily, 'Hi lover, some bloody nice friends you got.'

'You silly cow,' I said with my lips in her hair. 'You're not to be trusted on your own.' And I felt the pressure of her hand on my arm before Ginney was sitting up groggily and nursing his bruised jaw.

I was called to give evidence at Paul's trial for the attempted murder of Sandra Brinlett. Persuaded to plead guilty by his lawyers, he was permitted to ask for the assault on Arnold Plater to be taken into consideration. As I learned later, he was also dissuaded from saying that if I hadn't murdered his wife, none of this would have happened. An outburst wouldn't help him, he was told. Not this time. Not while the murder of his late wife was still on file and open.

He stared at me when I gave evidence of the bad blood between us being the reason for his following me to Brighton. When asked why I thought he'd attempt to murder Sandra, I wasn't allowed to answer and it was left to the prosecuting counsel to suggest his only interest in the victim was his desire to get me arrested for murder again.

With no clear idea of what I hoped would come out of it, I tried to find Sandra after the trial. I found that Ginney had arranged for her to be put in a police car and driven home to pack and slope off to pastures new. By that time he and I were quite good friends and when he said, 'It wouldn't have done, mate,' I knew he was right. After the defence had tried to get Leighton's sentence reduced by suggesting that Sandra approached him, took him to her room for sex, and then provoked him into attacking her, what chance would we have of a normal life? All you had to do was see what grabbed the next morning's headlines and how far down the page you had to go to find out that Paul got eight years.

After a time I cleaned up my act at work, learned to dust Margery's photograph, and cut out most of the booze. Crazy Bear stopped visiting, farting, and insulting me quite so often or at least, I didn't need him to. Vic and Joan took me back in their bosoms and started feeding me on Friday nights. From time to time, I thought about selling out to Bobby and moving on but like Ginney said, it would only mean another flat warming. I looked at him. He laughed and admitted that Delia had told him all about the first one.

Besides, he had a widowed sister who, he warned me, was so like him I'd probably be calling her sergeant when she gave the two of us a meal one evening.

I didn't call her sergeant. I looked at her neat figure and saw Margery, right down to the smile that seemed to hover constantly on her lips and the mid-brown hair that curled invitingly round her ears. I liked Barbara. Because, like me, she ate meat, I was able to take her to the restaurants Margery had liked and somehow, watching her grab the lioness' share and the familiar surroundings made it possible to watch her eat without a qualm.

'She's not a bit like you,' I told Ginney a few weeks later and after his sister and I had been to bed together. 'She doesn't have a broken nose and her moustache is smaller.'

'So when are you going to make a honest woman of her?' he asked, patting me on the arm.

I didn't know. I took her to visit Delia and Bobby and when my sister-in-law asked me the same question, I didn't know. Inevitably the day came when Barbara asked the same question. We were in my flat. I sat on the old sofa and ran my hand over the arm. I told her it wasn't about her. I couldn't marry because one day what happened to Margery or what happened to Sara could happen again. I couldn't let myself get that close to anyone again. I couldn't take the pain of losing her. My eyes were closed and it wasn't until I felt her fingers on my lips, I knew Barbara was sitting beside me.

'Sam was a copper,' she said. 'He was my husband, my lover, and my best friend for fifteen years. It was all ended in a night by an over tired Dutch trucker who forgot which side of the road he was supposed to be driving on. If I could have died for Sam, with him, or instead of him, I'd have grabbed the chance. But life doesn't work that way and I had to watch Sam die instead. The way you had to watch Margery die.'

Blindly I reached for her and for the first time since I lost my wife, I willingly let another person see me cry. And somehow, a little of the bitterness I'd been nurturing all those years began to ebb away.

We honeymooned in Chicago, getting to know each other and doing the tourist thing, Barbara insisting on visiting the Museum of Science and Industry and the butterflies at the Field, me insisting on seeing where Al Capone lived and where John Dillinger was shot down. Among our souvenirs, I bought two brown clay wall plaques, one of an Indian maid with braided hair and two feathers in her headband, the other of an Indian Chief. Noble, stubborn, beak nosed, long haired, and wearing full feathered headdress. Barbara named the maid Running Deer and the chief Geronimo. I watched Crazy Bear rein in his horse and throw back his head. Our laughter echoed off the Black Hills and the walls of the bedroom. Easy tears ran down my cheeks. And when my wife demanded to know the joke, I could only shake my head and take her in my arms.

~~ The End ~~

About the Author

Mark Rickman joined the army in 1943 as an eighteen-year-old infantryman. During his service in South East Asia Command he became interested in military history and uniforms. This led to work on costumes and equipment for films and TV productions such as *Becket, A Man For All Seasons, The Charge Of The Light Brigade, Camelot, Elizabeth R*, and of course, *Dr Who*.

Retired in his fifties, he has written short stories and articles for family and writers' magazines for thirty years and has been published by *Woman's Own, Woman and Home, Family Circle, Raconteur, Best, Bella, The New Writer, Amicus*, and many other weekly and monthly magazines, including sales to Norway and South Africa through an agent.

His Victorian crime novel *'Sarah Fowkes'* was short-listed for the 2002 Harry Bowling prize for novels about London. A short story *'Alec's Dog'* (about a man with severe learning difficulties) came joint second in the 2003 Allianz Cornhill competition, held at the Guildford Book Festival. His play *'The Day The Fish Walked'* won a third in the 2003 Sussex Playwrights one act play competition. Another play *'Soliloquies'* had a short season at the Blue Elephant theatre in Camberwell and was again featured as part of the Seven Oaks summer festival in 2004. In 2008, his story *Chicken Run* came third in the Earlyworks Press Gender Genre competition.

Circaidy Gregory

Independent Books for Independent Readers

Circaidy Gregory is a small press set up by Kay Green, writer, editor, and administrator of the Earlyworks Press Writers' and Reviewers' Club. Earlyworks Press exists to offer resources and good company to writers developing their careers and our imprint, Circaidy Gregory, is dedicated to the production of high quality, single author collections by writers we feel are going to appear in mainstream catalogues before too long.

Circaidy Gregory has so far produced four first collections by authors we have met through Earlyworks Press competitions and club activities. They are 'Light in the Shade' – short stories by Pam Eaves, who came to our attention after being short listed several times in Earlyworks Press fiction competitions; Kay Green's own 'Jung's People' which was originally published by Andrew Hook's award-winning Elastic Press; 'wormwood, earth and honey' – poems by Catherine Edmunds who was short listed in the Earlyworks Press High Fantasy Challenge, sci-fi and poetry competitions; and 'red silk slippers' by Marilyn Francis, a poet we met through club activities and who has also been short listed in several competitions. 'red silk slippers' is the latest addition to what we hope will be a growing list of poetry that is fresh, accessible and intelligent.

Circaidy Gregory is also building an impressive list of novels, which began with 'Charity's Child' – an unputdownable story by Rosalie Warren, who was short listed in the Science Fiction Challenge and whose story 'Touching the Rabbit' caused a stir in the 'Gender Genre' Challenge which 'Crazy Bear' author Mark Rickman was also shortlisted in. 'Charity's Child' has proved a great success with library reading groups and Rosalie has since gone on to secure a contract with a larger publisher. New additions in 2009 were Cathy Edmunds' MR novel 'Small Poisons' and now 'Crazy Bear'.

Circaidy Gregory Press offers rewarding, unusual finds to readers who have high standards and enjoy searching out something just that little bit different. To find out more about our authors, and our plans for the future, please visit our website…

www.circaidygregory.co.uk

Small Poisons

Catherine Edmunds

A contemporary novel for Midsummer Night's Dreamers

With charm, wit and magical style
Catherine Edmunds conjures a
fairy tale for grown ups, in a place
where dreams and stark reality
meet.

- Neil Marr, BeWrite Books

Small Poisons by Catherine Edmunds UK £9.50
Pub Circaidy Gregory Press ISBN 978 1 906451 16 5

Charity's Child
Rosalie Warren

Dark deed or virgin birth?

Who is the father of Charity's Child? 16-year-old Charity Baker has her own crazy ideas but even her loyal friend Joanne finds them hard to believe.

As the story reaches its disturbing climax, darkness is revealed in unexpected places and we learn with Joanna that many things in Charity's life are not as they seem.

This powerful tale of teenage sexuality, religious fanaticism, self-harm and other highly topical issues has proved a popular reading group choice, shedding a much-needed light on the experience of the younger generation in modern Britain.

Charity's Child by Rosalie Warren UK £9.50
Pub Circaidy Gregory Press ISBN 978 1 906451 07 3